G000129975

THE
HAR

BY TRUMAN CAPOTE

★

★

DRAMATISTS
PLAY SERVICE
INC.

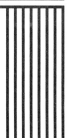

THE GRASS HARP was first presented by Saint-Subber in association with Rita Allen at the Martin Beck Theatre, New York City, on March 27, 1952. The play was directed by Robert Lewis and scenery and costumes were designed by Cecil Beaton. The cast was as follows:

CATHERINE CREEK ....Georgia Burke
COLLIN TALBO ....Johnny Stewart
DOLLY TALBO ....Mildred Natwick
VERENA TALBO ....Ruth Nelson
DR. MORRIS RITZ ....Jonathan Harris
THE REVEREND'S WIFE ....Susan Steell
THE REVEREND ....Ralph Hertz
THE BARBER ....Sterling Holloway
THE BAKER'S WIFE ....Gertrude Flynn
THE POSTMASTER ....Jay Barney
THE SHERIFF ....Val Dufour
JUDGE CHARLIE COOL ....Russell Collins
THE CHOIR MISTRESS ....Jane Smith
BIG EDDIE STOVER ....Anthony McGrath
BROPHY ....Jules Racine
SAM ....Larry Robinson
MAUDE RIORDAN ....Lenka Peterson
MISS BABY LOVE DALLAS ....Alice Pearce

SYNOPSIS OF SCENES

ACT I

SCENE 1. The Talbo house. A Sunday afternoon in late September.
SCENE 2. The town. The following morning.
SCENE 3. An autumn wood. The same day.

ACT II

SCENE 1. The wood. Early the following morning and that night.
SCENE 2. The Talbo house. That evening.

The Play Service hereby acknowledges with grateful thanks the friendly help of Mr. Ben Kranz, production stage manager of the Broadway production, for his help in preparing this acting edition.

3

SUGGESTIONS FOR SIMPLIFIED STAGING

The description of the set of the Talbo house in Act I, Scene 1 calls for a painted drop at the front of the stage, representing the exterior of the house. This drop is made chiefly of scrim, and as soon as the lights go up behind it, it is seen to be transparent, and the dining room interior is seen through the scrim. However, while such a drop does add to the effectiveness of the set, it is not essential. This set could be built wholly as an interior if desired. If that is done, the Talbo house set would consist only of the dining room. The sidewalk and front of the house would be eliminated, and all actors' entrances from outside the house would be made at the Up Right door of the dining room. The stage directions that appear in this text would still apply, only eliminating all movements for actors that precede their appearance at the Up Right dining room door. This omits only the walking across the sidewalk in front of the house and entering at the front stoop.

The woods set for Act I, Scene 3 and Act II, Scene 1 need not be elaborate. A very simple, stylized tree trunk with some branches spreading out from it should dominate the stage. A few boards nailed together to suggest a raft in the crotch of the tree would suffice for the tree house. That, with some rocks for a fireplace Down Right and a mound Down Left, could complete the scenery. The grass shown Up Right in the photograph of this set adds to the effect, but is not necessary. A painted backdrop can be used for this set, but it, also, is not essential.

MUSIC

The music used in the original Broadway production of THE GRASS HARP was composed by Virgil Thomson. Producing groups interested in this music should contact Boosey & Hawkes, 35 East 21st Street, New York, NY 10010. Attn: Carolyn Kalett. Phone: 212-358-5350. Fax: 212-358-5305.

THE GRASS HARP

ACT I

SCENE 1

A Sunday afternoon late in September.

WE SEE: *The Talbo house—a painted drop at front of stage, extremely stylized, representing the dull-tinted exterior of the house. The larger part of the drop screening the room behind it, is of scrim. All the drop is scrim except the extreme* R. *and* L. *sides, and the upper half of it which represents the second story of the house—these parts cannot be seen through. The house is two-story, with four second-story windows and with ground-floor windows. Into this drop, at extreme* D. R., *and a little above the level of the stage, a small front stoop, or one or two steps are provided, leading to a practical front door. Space must be allowed on the apron of the stage, below the curtain line where the painted drop falls, at least three feet wide, all the way across the stage. This is the sidewalk, and is so used in Act 1, Scene 1 and in Act 11, Scene 2. As the play begins, only the front walk and the painted drop with the front stoop and door are seen. For a few moments, until the audience are able to familiarize themselves with what is visible to them, music may play. At the proper moment the music fades, then that part of the drop that is scrim begins to light up, the interior behind it becomes visible, and it is seen to be a dining room. The appearance of the dining room, seen through the scrim, is, as it were, a picture framed by the part of the drop which is not scrim, and embedded there, like the scenes inside of sugar Easter eggs. The front door in the exterior drop* D. R. *leads into an entrance hall, which is not seen by the audience, as it is concealed by the non-scrim section of the drop. People entering the house go in the D. R. front door, up the hall-way—unseen by the audience—and next appear through the door that leads from the hallway into the dining room. This door is placed U. R. in the R. wall of the dining room. In the back wall of the dining room there are two moderately large windows, hung with pink and gold-tasselled draperies. Between the windows is a spindly cabinet with Victorian gewgaws. At the L., in the rear wall of the dining room, is the kitchen door, a swinging door, which is open, revealing an impressionistic glimpse of the kitchen: linoleum, the pan-littered black end of an old-style stove. A pink rose-patterned paper covers the walls of the dining room. Many pictures, daguerreotype portraits, paintings of oversized fruit and flowers, vege-tables, of fowls and huge fish, are hung in peculiar posi-tions—as though the purpose had been to obscure various stains. D. R., along the R. wall, is a mahogany sideboard. There are at least three spindly glass cabinets here and there, filled with crystal and china of various kinds. One, above referred to, stands between the windows, another is against the R. wall, just above the U. R. door. A rubber plant, or possibly a palm stands in one corner—U. L. A cuckoo clock decorates the R. wall above the sideboard. The focus of the room, the dining table, one capable of seating six people, is situated C. stage. Suspended above it there is a crystal and ruby glass chandelier. A fish bowl filled with water and inhabited by a solitary and enormous goldfish, occupies a prominent part of the table. Chairs stand at the head and foot of the table, and two are placed by the upstage side of the table. A fire-place with a large ornate mantel occupies most of the L. wall of the dining room. There is a chair above the mantel and a chair below it, both against the L. wall. On the wall above the mantel is a large mirror. On the mantel are two candles in candlesticks.*

As the lights come up on the dining room, the figure of Collin Talbo is seen standing at the chair below the mantel. He is a sturdy, well-made yet rather homely-faced boy of about fifteen. He wears a white shirt with rolled-up sleeves and a pair of khaki summer trousers.

He strikes a match to light a cigarette, tosses the match over his head, and lazily moves above the dining table to the upstage window at R. After a moment at the window he moves down toward the table. Catherine Creek is seated in one of the chairs above the table. She is a Negress, chunky and rough-voiced, and appears to be dressed for a party. She wears a fancy calico dress, in one hand she clutches a handkerchief. A turquoise necklace is strung around her neck, her ears are studded with turquoise earrings, six of her fingers are loaded with rings. She is working a jigsaw puzzle which is spread on the table before her. Collin sits on chair at R. of table. At this point the preliminary music ends.

CATHERINE. It's a good thing you got your growth, because now you'd stunt it for sure: smoking and dancing and floozies—those are among the several things that will stunt a boy's growth and drive him crazy.

COLLIN. I don't know any floozies.

CATHERINE. (*Frowning worriedly at goldfish bowl.*) Buster's eyes look right swollen: always staring—what does he find to look at so much? (*Then to Collin.*) You don't know anything but floozies. (*She fits a piece of the jigsaw puzzle.*) Except for Dollyheart: and naturally myself. There is no such thing as an Indian floozy.

COLLIN. Exactly now—which side of your family were Indians?

CATHERINE. All sides. I've told you so one hundred and fifty thousand times. Why don't you stop lolling around and spend your energies in a profitable manner?

COLLIN. (*Stubbing out his cigarette on the sole of his shoe and dropping butt into the cuff of his trousers.*) Yeah? Why don't you?

CATHERINE. (*Indignantly.*) Who feeds you, Collin Talbo? Washes and irons and darns your clothes? and totes your slopjar?

COLLIN. (*Rocking back in his chair so that it is balanced on its rear legs.*) Dolly.

CATHERINE. (*With a crestfallen shrug.*) Well—Dolly and me, it's the same thing. It's just that I've got to be particular: things catch me here—(*She grabs the small of her back.*) and here. (*Thumps her chest and coughs.*) But what I say is, why don't you

7

get a hammer and nails and build a chicken-coop? Or learn the French language?

COLLIN. (*Bored.*) Uh huh. Why don't you? Instead of wasting your life on jigsaw puzzles.

CATHERINE. I *know* the French language. You recall that winter three winters ago Dolly and me improved us-selves? *Je suis fatiguée*—that's all I need to know. But a man and ladies are different.

COLLIN. No foolin'. What did you do—read that in the paper?

CATHERINE. (*Thoughtfully.*) A man should be a scholar and brood about business. A lady, like Verena, like That One, she is not a lady. Mind you, I'm the first to give That One credit—if you sit down and think about it we nearly own this town; and every bit of it is That One's doing. (*Collin, bored, gets up, moves to window* R. *Catherine shakes head, heaves a disgruntled sigh.*) But you surely can't say the earning of it, all the property and all, you can't say it's made her an easy woman! (*Mimicking.*) Who left the water running in the bathroom? Which one of you broke my umbrella? Dolly, you get rid of that kitten, you want to aggravate my asthma? . . . (*Breaks off exasperatedly. During Catherine's speech, Collin has his back to the audience, gently taps his fingertips against the glass.*) And like today—hollering at us to kill all the chickens and plow up the vegetable garden, all on account of this little Dr. Morris Ritz is coming for Sunday supper. . . .

COLLIN. (*Remaining at window.*) But just who is he? Old Dr. Morris Ritz?

CATHERINE. You haven't seen him slinkin' along the street like a lizard? Only what he's a doctor of and what his credentials are, that is a mystery. (*She fits a puzzle piece.*) This I do know: him and That One are up to something in the business line. I can smell it. She met him in Chicago last July when she was there on that buying trip—then suddenly three days ago he pops up here in town living at the Lola Hotel. Twenty-five years we've lived in this house and That One has asked maybe exactly two gentlemen to take a meal here—so naturally I was considerable surprised when she says this morning fry up all the chickens and shell all the peas and dust all the china and iron all the linen and—lord-amercy! (*Pounding jigsaw in place.*) on account of Dr. Morris Ritz is coming to Sunday supper (*The piece does not fit, so she*

8

tears it to make it fit and places it in puzzle.) I said Miss Verena, well, I said, I'm innerested to know now who is this funny-looking little Dr. Morris Ritz. And That One, she says, getting all white around the mouth, well, sir, he's not so funny looking as *some* I could name. . . . (*Unnoticed by Collin or Catherine, Dolly Talbo has, during the last third of the preceding speech, appeared in the kitchen doorway* U. L., *then, as Collin laughs at Catherine's concluding lines, she comes into the room with a swift fragile-footed quietness, her presence is a delicate happening. She is a small pretty woman. Her movements are quick and yet uncertain, it disturbs her to make the most ordinary decision—whether to place a saucer here, a fork there. She is wearing a white, virginal, almost ankle-length dress and a somewhat frayed pink apron. She is carrying an elaborate bowl of roses.*)

DOLLY. Hush now, hush. (*She waves, not knowing where to put roses.*) Hush now. Poking fun at Verena. (*Deposits roses on sideboard.*) Supposing she heard you? I will not tolerate having anyone hurt her feelings. She works very hard to provide the comforts you enjoy . . . that we all enjoy. In her own home she should have a sense of peace and affection.

CATHERINE. I'm affectionate. I have an affectionate nature. But Dollyheart, dear child, you are not blind to the fact that That One has a cold place in herself concerning myself. About today—she says Catherine I spec you better wear a nice uniform for when Dr. Ritz comes to dinner. Now, Dollyheart, you know it's not that I exactly object to being mistook for common kitchen help . . . besides which That One has never laid out to buy me uniforms. Here's what she said: Trot over and borrow one off Mrs. Redfern's Ginger Jones. To humiliate myself before Ginger Jones!

DOLLY. (*Counting silver and collecting table linen for two place settings from drawers of sideboard, places it on top of sideboard.*) Hush now. Hush.

CATHERINE. —as if me and Ginger Jones wore the same fit. You could wrap up this table in a pair of her step-ins. She must weigh . . . Collin, sugar, what would you say is Ginger Jones' weight?

COLLIN. (*Absent-mindedly, still gazing out window.*) How much she weighs? Something like the same as you.

CATHERINE. (*Grimly.*) That's inneresting. That's an inneresting piece of observing. I see you forget that you are obliged to me for the mere circumstances of having grown to ordinary human size. If it wasn't for my treatments you'd still be a little runt like Biddy Skinner . . . and folks tell how he's had offers from the circus. But I took pity: oh, yes, I pulled at your legs and tugged at your head until inside of two years I'd stretched you from four-foot nine to five-foot seven . . .

COLLIN. Jesus, Catherine, you ask me how much somebody weighs. For Christ's sake . . .

DOLLY. (*Hands over her ears.*) Please. This is Sunday: it's so important to toe the line. And, Collin . . . while I remember . . . Verena is upset that you didn't go to church this morning. I told her that you had a pain. So do try to look as though you were in some sort of agony. (*Collin staggers with cross-eyed abandon away from windows, leans on dining table.*) Not drunk, dear: in agony. (*Suddenly, from sideboard drawers where she is selecting linen and silver, she lifts a paper sack containing jelly beans.*) Fancy this . . . my bag of jellybeans; really, I'd looked everywhere. (*She nibbles at one, then drops it back in sack.*) They do seem a bit mouldy. Catherine . . . you've always wanted to get some colored pebbles for Buster's bowl. And these are just like pebbles—(*She advances to goldfish bowl.*) and such lovely colors . . .

CATHERINE. (*Clamps a protective hand over bowl.*) Hold off! Buster here, he'd go for those jellies like a shark. It's not like he was young: you got to watch his diet.

DOLLY. (*As though reminded.*) Diet . . . I had a letter from Mr. Culver Joy. (*Searching in dress-pockets under her apron, she produces several envelopes.*)

CATHERINE. Mr. Culver Joy from Joy City? That's one of our best customers. (*Collin moves above table to Dolly.*) This is from his granddaughter. Says: (*She reads.*) "Dear Miss Dolly Talbo . . . we appreciate all the grand work your dropsy cure medicine did for our granddaddy but we will not be needing any more bottles as, Bless His Soul, he passed away night before last. He would eat pork and that's what did it. . . ." (*Looking up.*) I told them not to feed that man any pork. Specifically I said no pork or greasy foods. And not any sugar . . .

CATHERINE. (*Piously.*) There's no blame can be attached to us, Dollyheart. We did our best. He was tempted. (*Then with genuine *melancholy.*) But gracious knows it's a big loss; he's been a standing order three years. Mr. Culver Joy.

DOLLY. Now there's somebody new. For instance—(*Unfolds another letter.*) here's a Mrs. Clyde W. Dwyer: she lives in Arrow Springs.

COLLIN. (*Reading letter he has taken from her.*) "Dear Miss Talbo. I have the dropsy something terrible and have tried many remedies that have lessened my complaint not one whit. Word has reached me that you brew a homemade dropsy cure that beats all. Kindly send me a trial bottle. It surely will do me good if my husband doesn't get at it first: he is a devil drunkard who will drink anything."

DOLLY. (*Eagerly.*) Where does it say that . . . that last part? . . . (*Collin laughs, and Dolly, seeing it is a joke, playfully swats at him as he moves away to L. of table. She puts letters back in her pocket.*) But that makes eight new orders: we'll have to make two trips to the woods this week. I want to get enough herbs to carry us through the winter. Why . . . do look at that —— (*She means the cuckoo clock above sideboard.*) Collin honey, look in the kitchen and call me the time. Says twelve. . . . I wonder, did it stop at midnight or at noon? (*She drags her chair over to sideboard. As Collin exits into kitchen, Dolly climbs on chair R., to fiddle with clock.*)

COLLIN. (*Offstage.*) Half-past four.

CATHERINE. (*Calling to Collin.*) I'll skin you if you gobble them chicken-livers. You know Dollyheart won't touch nothing but them chicken-livers.

COLLIN. (*Entering from kitchen. He lifts Dolly off chair, whirls and swings her to floor, singing:*)
> Roses are red, violets are blue,
> Sugar is sweet and so are you.

(*Dolly gently touches Collin's cheek, and with other hand reaches toward Catherine, who takes it. There is a gentle moment of love expressed in these gestures.*)

DOLLY. But four-thirty! And the table not even set! . . . Clear away that jigsaw. (*Grabbing tablecloth from sideboard, shaking it out and replacing chair at R. of table.*) . . . and, Collin, go brush your teeth, put some shine on your shoes . . .

CATHERINE. (*Calmly thwarting Dolly's attempts to arrange tablecloth.*) Hold off . . . I've been working at this jigsaw going

11

on nine days. There's only maybe two dozen piece left. Give me a hand, Dollyheart, let's see what the picture is.

COLLIN. It's a windmill . . . and tulips . . . and those wooden shoes . . . (*Verena Talbo enters* D. L. *along sidewalk outside house. She is dressed in black and gray, she wears gloves and carries above her a black parasol. Her hat is black straw decorated with a gray dove. She has tucked under her arm a small paper-wrapped parcel. A small woman giving an impression of height, she walks as though she were part of a slow and haughty procession: her posture is severe, her manner exalted. During this entrance the scene in the dining room has continued: which is to say, there has been no interruption of dialogue.*)

DOLLY. (*Holding a handful of puzzle pieces.*) Here's an eye. Blue. Anyone there with a missing blue eye?

CATHERINE. Honey, there's whole hands missing.

DOLLY. (*Looks at clock, at just this moment Verena is half-way between* L. *and* R. *stage on sidewalk.*) . . . we won't have any heads either if Sister . . . This belongs there. (*She tries to jam into place a piece of the puzzle.*)

CATHERINE. (*Wrenching it out.*) No it don't. It's the wrong shape entirely. Look for a little wiggly piece.

DOLLY. (*Sorting the pieces.*) Wiggly? (*Meantime Verena, having crossed to outside door* D. R., *folds her umbrella, has entered, goes* U. R. *through passageway. The* U. R. *door of the dining room opens. It is Verena, who enters, still wearing her hat and carrying the paper parcel. The umbrella has been left in the hallway. The others do not immediately look at her, they tense with an awareness of her presence, then Collin moves again toward windows upstage as if to escape the range of her gaze. Dolly smooths her hands on her apron and turns to face Verena.*) Sister . . . we didn't expect . . . Is our guest here? Everything . . . (*She glances at clock.*) everything is ready . . . almost.

VERENA. (*Advancing to table and putting her parcel there, then slowly pulling out the long pins that fasten her hat.*) Yes. Yes. Your efforts are evident. (*A sarcastic pause, she takes off her hat and jabs the pins into the brim.*) Get that nonsense off my table. (*She sweeps jigsaw puzzle pieces onto the floor, not with fury—rather, a serene casual impatience. Dolly hesitates an instant, presently she stoops and begins gathering up the puzzle, dropping its pieces into the fold of her apron. Collin helps her, but Cath-*

erine, sitting with averted head, works her lips in a ceaseless, soundless cursing. Verena puts her hat, gloves, and coat on a chair beside the mantel.)

DOLLY. (As she is picking up puzzle.) Everything is ready, Verena. We were just about to set the table. Do peek in the kitchen . . . there's going to be fried chicken and ham. English peas. Rolls. Banana pudding. (Her voice ascends with enthusiasm.) Two kinds of cake and tuttifrutti ice cream from the drugstore.

VERENA. (Ignoring Dolly. To Catherine.) I've brought you a uniform. (She slides parcel on table toward Catherine.) You will go to your room and scrape the paint off your face. You will bathe . . . I cannot have you smelling like a sow in the spring. You will clean under your fingernails and remove the jewelry: this is a private home, not a café.

CATHERINE. (She has not and never will look at Verena directly.) I'm no kin to you. I'm no kin to you.

DOLLY. (Rising from floor where she has finished collecting the pieces, and hands puzzle to Catherine.) Hush. Hush now.

CATHERINE. Hush. Hush. (She gets up from her chair and picks up goldfish bowl, holding it in the crook of one arm.) It's not me you're telling to hush: it's you, Dollyheart, it's yourself. Hush. (She slaps her hand against her heart, she moves toward kitchen door, repeating "hush, hush," each time striking her heart.)

VERENA. (Imperturbably removing her gloves.) The uniform.

DOLLY. (Taking parcel from table, carrying it to Catherine.) Please . . . (Catherine accepts parcel and exits into kitchen. Dolly begins to set table for dinner. Simultaneously Collin is more or less sneaking toward dining room U. R. door, which has been open since Verena's entrance. But Verena has eyes in the back of her head—she "sees" him.)

VERENA. Collin . . . were you excused?

COLLIN. (From the U. R. door's threshold.) Yes, ma'am.

VERENA. Yes, ma'am?

COLLIN. Yes, ma'am, I wasn't excused.

VERENA. You were not in church?

COLLIN. (Exchanging an apprehensive glance with Dolly.) I had, gee, an awful toothache. . . .

VERENA. (Turning to give him an appraising look.) Then it shall be taken out. I will call Dr. Skinner this evening.

13

COLLIN. Well, it wasn't altogether my *tooth* . . . stomach gripes . . .

VERENA. I shouldn't wonder . . . at your age, the drinking you do. All those roadhouses on the highway? I've a mind to have the proprietors jailed. But, Collin, my dear, it is simply later than you know. I won't always be able to stand between you . . . and the penitentiary.

DOLLY. (*She has been distractedly setting table.*) Oh, Verena! Sister!

VERENA. But one thing is certain. Maude Riordan's papa has denounced to me your conduct with his daughter. Is it true you shine flashlights in her window at night? And throw pebbles? And tempt her into the yard?

COLLIN. I have a right to. She's my girl friend.

VERENA. That will stop.

COLLIN. My particular girl friend.

VERENA. (*Her hand twitching in a gesture of disgust and dismissal.*) Take these with you and leave them in the hall on the hat-tree. (*She means her hat, coat and gloves, which are lying on a chair beside the mantel, he comes forward to collect them as she picks them up, but holds on to them.*) And, Collin, at least today behave as though you were a gentleman. . . . I know how difficult that will be considering certain inheritances . . . (*She releases her hold on the clothes and Collin starts for* U. R. *door.*) but . . . I value Dr. Ritz's esteem.

COLLIN. Yes, ma'am. (*Exits through the* U. R. *dining-room door. Verena seats herself in chair at* L. *of table, though she closes her eyes and folds her hands, her posture is rigid and her knees primly together. The light at the windows and in the room has deepened, is bluer, and Dolly, who previously has taken two candlesticks from mantel and put them on the table, now lights them.*)

DOLLY. (*Has set the table during this dialogue with linen, two place settings and a small silver dinner bell.*) I wish you wouldn't scold him so . . . nor say what you do about "inheritance": he knows you mean his father . . .

VERENA. (*Her eyes closed and her voice distant.*) He should be reminded.

DOLLY. How reminded, Sister? That they're dead: his mother Mary, our cousin Mary, such a pretty, pretty, pretty girl . . .

14

VERENA. He killed her . . . with his trips and his drinking and his women . . .

DOLLY. She loved him. Mary would not have loved anyone really wicked.

VERENA. Hateful man. Hateful.

DOLLY. (*Going to sideboard for bowl of roses.*) But he's dead . . .

VERENA. Most opportunely . . . he owed me eleven hundred and forty-three dollars.

DOLLY. (*Placing roses between the burning candles in candlesticks in C. of table.*) I was against Collin coming here . . . it seemed wrong, raising a boy in a houseful of women. I feel differently now: maybe because I'm selfish and wouldn't like the sound of this house without Collin in it. Anyway I don't worry: I know he'll get on, he'll make his mark. Because he's smart, so much smarter than Catherine or me.

VERENA. That, of course, is claiming a great deal. Smart. As I remember, he was in the fifth grade two years—and now they won't even allow him *in* the schoolhouse!

DOLLY. And good. You're so taken up, oh, you've never seen him, Sister . . . when he would come from the outdoors in the cold weather and his cheeks like this—(*She cups a rose in her hand.*) and fill himself with a bushel of biscuits. And when we go to the woods to hunt our herbs he knows where the pennyroyal is, and the best sweetmary. A boy who knows such things is good, Verena: he'll get on . . .

VERENA. (*Wearily.*) Do be still a moment.

DOLLY. (*Coming behind Verena, gently resting her fingertips on Verena's temples.*) You *are* tired, Sister. It worries me every night when I wake and see the light still burning under your door. And I wonder, Verena . . . why not close your ledgers, sell the stores? We could have long mornings drinking coffee in the kitchen.

VERENA. Oh, Dolly . . . That's what I promised Papa . . . promised him to protect you, make it possible for you to sit long mornings in the kitchen with your puzzles and your jokes. Sit in the kitchen: that's for women and children. (*With wistful longing.*) I wouldn't know how. (*Suddenly staring at table, then standing up.*) Why have you set only two places?

DOLLY. (*Her head lowered, mumbling.*) I thought we . . . Collin and myself . . . we would eat in the kitchen with Catherine.

VERENA. (*Goes to sideboard and returns, bringing additional plates and silver for two more place settings, with which she proceeds to reset table.*) Don't fool with me, Dolly; don't tax me. This is important. Dr. Ritz is coming here expressly to meet you.

DOLLY. To meet me?

VERENA. What is more, I'd appreciate it if you'd hold up your head: it makes me dizzy, hanging like that. (*Dr. Morris Ritz enters in the same manner as Verena—from L.—along sidewalk to R. then to outside door D. R. A skinny, dagger-faced man with a slick small moustache, his clothes have the checkered gaudiness of a race-tout's, and he walks with a jazzy cockiness, all the while snapping his fingers and whistling.*)

DOLLY. (*Deeply disturbed*) But . . . he will look at me. I couldn't, I can't . . . (*Front door bell rings: it is Dr. Ritz, who has reached the front door. At the sound of it Dolly, looking terrified, skitters around table, as if hunting a corner to hide. Verena tries to halt her, but she escapes and rushes through kitchen door. Meanwhile, front door is opened for Dr. Ritz by Collin. Collin has put on a jacket and tie.*)

RITZ. (*Laughing: his laughter is like a nervous disorder.*) Ha ha —uh—ladies of the house at home? Ritz is the name. (*Collin steps silently aside for Ritz, then closes door. They go up the hall and in an instant we see them enter the dining-room where Verena, falsely composed and smiling, advances to shake his hand.*)

VERENA. Ah, Morris . . . so good of you. Have you met Collin? Collin is my poor cousin Mary's boy. He lives with us. (*Ritz laughs and slaps Collin on the back; at the same time his eyes are shrewdly swerving about the room.*)

RITZ. Real old family mansion you got hold of here, Verena. Pretty ritzy. Ritz: ritzy. Ha ha.

VERENA. My sister is so anxious to meet you. (*Calling toward kitchen door.*) Dolly . . . Dolly, dear. (*After a pause she calls more sternly.*) I say, Dolly!

CATHERINE. (*Poking her head out kitchen door.*) Dolly's flat on her back. Her bowels is bad. (*She withdraws.*)

RITZ. (*Nervously.*) Ha ha. Ha ha.

VERENA. Collin —— (*Motions him toward kitchen door. He stifles a laugh as he moves to door and exits.*)

RITZ. (*To Verena: not whispering, but in a subdued, somewhat conspiratorial manner*.) Well, my dear, have you . . . uh . . . broached the matter?

VERENA. (*Shakes head, looks troubled, then.*) Not yet. I don't want her to think we're taking anything away from her. It is for her own ultimate good. . . . (*Shakes head again.*) Such a fearful burden to be the only grownup in a houseful of children: they have no one to depend on except me . . . and I have no one except myself.

RITZ. (*Taking Verena's hand.*) You can depend on me, Verena.

VERENA. Someone else told me that once. (*Looking at him.*) I believe you. If I didn't . . .

RITZ. But we must get the recipe. I've had answers from three firms in Chicago, ready to place orders on the basis of the samples we sent them.

VERENA. (*Harassed, excited, almost whispering.*) All right. All right. I will, Morris . . . now . . . today . . . (*Kitchen door opens and Collin, with a coaxing gesture, brings Dolly into the room. Verena, as she takes Dolly's hand and pulls her forward to meet Ritz, smiling.*) Dolly dear, this is our guest. . . . Dr. Morris Ritz from Chicago.

RITZ. (*Offering his hand.*) A rare pleasure, to be sure. . . . (*Dolly shyly gives her hand to Ritz, who kisses it in a far too obvious manner.*)

VERENA. Morris, will you sit here next to Collin. (*The seating arrangement at table is as follows: Ritz and Collin side by side facing audience, Dolly and Verena in profile at either end of the table. To Ritz.*) I hope you don't expect more than plain home food . . . very plain, I'm afraid. (*Rings small silver dinner bell.*)

DOLLY. (*As though suddenly wakened.*) Oh, but it's a lovely dinner today, Sister. (*She looks at Ritz.*) With tuttifrutti from the drugstore and two kinds of cake, and banana pudding . . .

RITZ. (*With a sickly expression.*) No sweets for me. (*Catherine enters through kitchen door with a platter of fried chicken. She has not removed her jewelry. She is wearing the uniform Verena brought her—it is blue and fits her like a sausage-skin, the skirt is hiked well above her knees. She serves Dolly first, then offers the platter to Ritz, who examines chicken dubiously.*) Tell you the truth, the only piece of chicken I can digest is the liver. Don't suppose you'd have that back in the kitchen, Mammy?

17

CATHERINE. (*Menacingly.*) Dollyheart's done took them livers on her plate. (*Serves Verena and Collin.*)

DOLLY. (*Embarrassed, handing her plate to him.*) But let me pass them to you.

VERENA. She wants only sweet things anyway. You've noticed that the whole house smells of vanilla extract? Of course that's partly because Dolly wears it as a cologne.

RITZ. (*Changing plates with Dolly.*) If you're sure you don't mind . . . (*Sneezes explosively.*) Those roses . . . old allergy . . . kachoo!

DOLLY. (*Seizing roses and carrying them to sideboard.*) I am sorry . . . it never struck me you could catch anything from roses.

CATHERINE. (*Exiting into kitchen.*) You can't.

COLLIN. (*Gnawing a chicken leg and addressing Ritz.*) Excuse me. I'm interested. Do you cut people open?

RITZ. (*Whimpering.*) Cut people . . . ? (*Catherine enters from kitchen with a vegetable bowl and a cake on a plate, hereafter she will move back and forth between kitchen and dining-room, carelessly overloading table with various dishes.*)

VERENA. How nasty, Collin. Morris isn't that kind of a doctor . . . he's a pharmacist. (DOLLY *crosses to windows, draws the gold-tasseled draperies against the deep dusk.*)

RITZ. I'm what you could . . . uh . . . call a chemical engineer.

DOLLY. (*Turning from windows.*) You make medicines? We make a medicine. Collin and Catherine and me. We have customers all over the state.

RITZ. Why, sure, Miss Dolly . . . that dropsy cure of yours is a famous product. (*He and Verena exchange meaningful glances.*)

DOLLY. (*Disbelieving.*) Truly? You've heard of it?

RITZ. Would I kid you? (*Catherine, returning to kitchen, pauses in doorway. She stands there alertly listening.*) But tell me now, Miss Dolly . . . between you and me . . . what kind of stuff are you putting in this dropsy cure? (*Glancing again at Verena.*) It sorta, you might say, defies the analyzing methods of modern science.

DOLLY. (*Flattered but coy.*) A little of this, and well, a pinch of that . . .

CATHERINE. (*Proudly.*) That's Dollyheart's own secret. Don't nobody, not me or Collin or nobody, we don't know all of it that goes into the dropsy.

DOLLY. (*Shyly.*) It *is* a secret. I . . . I learned it from the gypsies.

VERENA. (*With forced sweetness.*) Dear, do tell Morris that old story of yours . . . about the gypsies.

DOLLY. (*She is standing, she rests her hands on back of chair in which she has previously been sitting and begins the story in a manner that is at first self-conscious, then gradually less so, she loses herself, her voice widens.*) Once . . . once when we were children . . . Verena with her babyteeth and Catherine no higher than a fence-post . . . there were gypsies thick as birds in a blackberry patch: not like now, when maybe you see a few straggling through each year. They came with spring: sudden, like the dogwood pink, there they were . . . up and down the road and in the woods around. But our men hated the sight of them. Papa said he would shoot any he caught on our place. And so I never told when I saw the gypsies taking water from the creek or stealing old winter pecans off the ground. (*Hesitates, clasps her hands together.*) Then one evening, it was April and raining, I went out to the cowshed where Fairybell had a new little calf. And there in the cowshed were three gypsy women, two of them old and one of them young, and the young one was lying na—(*She stutters. She glances at Ritz with embarrassment.*) naked and twisting on the cornshucks . . .

VERENA. Not that. Not all that. I mean about the medicine.

DOLLY. (*So concentrated she has not noticed the interruption.*) . . . When they saw that I was not afraid, that I was not going to run and tell, one of the old women asked would I bring a light. So I went to the house for a candle, and when I came back the woman who had sent me was holding a red little hollering baby upside down by its feet, and the other woman was milking Fairybell. I helped them wash the baby in the warm milk and wrap it in a scarf. (*She sinks into her chair and, as though she were offering it to a fortune-teller, holds out her palm.*) Then one of the old women took my hand and said: "Now I am going to give you a gift by teaching you a rhyme." It was a rhyme about evergreen bark, dragonfly fern . . . and all the other things that Collin and Catherine help me find in the woods: (*She chants.*) "Boil till dark and pure if you want a dropsy cure!" (*As though coming out of a trance, she looks at the others around the table, her voice grows self-conscious again.*) In the morning they were gone, the gypsies. I looked for them in the fields and on the road. There was nothing left of them but the rhyme in my head.

RITZ. (*Dreamily.*) Gypsy Queen Dropsy Cure . . . it's a natural! (*Cle..rs his throat.*) But, Miss Dolly, how do you go about making it, what's your process?

CATHERINE. That's Dollyheart's secret.

VERENA. Very well, Catherine. Kindly close the door. (*Catherine reaches behind her, slams kitchen door closed.*) With yourself behind it. (*Catherine exits to kitchen, presently she opens door a crack and we see her listening.*)

RITZ. (*To Dolly.*) You were saying . . . ?

DOLLY. (*Slicing for herself a piece of cake.*) Well . . . most every Saturday we go to the woods. Those are the River Woods down past the field of Indian grass. We have a tree-house. (*She picks crumbs off cake and pecks at them like a bird.*) Collin will tell you about the tree-house; he built it . . .

COLLIN. (*With an ashamed shrug.*) It's a tree-house . . .

DOLLY. (*Carried away.*) Oh, but a beautiful tree-house . . . like a raft floating in the leaves: so cool in the summer, and now in the fall, when you can hear the wind through the Indian grass and with the colors so fine . . . I really could live there. (*Ritz titters nervously, fingering his bow tie. Gives Verena a strained, inquiring glance. Verena, in a mood of mounting impatience, purses her lips, drums her fingers on table.*) We have picnics in the tree; then we hunt for herbs. The secret ones, the ones that make a difference. I find those myself. (*Proudly.*) We get a dollar a bottle, divided between us three ways. . . .

VERENA. (*Bunching her napkin and throwing it on table.*) Stop. Just stop. (*Dolly, startled, lets fall back onto the plate a batch of cake crumbs. Collin, too, stares at Verena, and Catherine, opening kitchen door wider, leans halfway into the room. Verena is breathing deeply and recovering a degree of composure.*) Without any further deviation, list for Morris the ingredients of . . . the drop ——

RITZ. (*Fervently, as though he already sees this trademark on a thousand billboards.*) The Gypsy Queen Dropsy Cure!

VERENA. That is what we want to know.

DOLLY. (*Bewildered.*) I don't understand, Sister. You never

20

cared about it before. Except you always said there would be trouble if we poisoned somebody. (*Lowers her head, almost whispers.*) Is it because you're afraid we'll poison somebody?

VERENA. (*Rising, she walks around table, moving slowly, and as though she is planning what she will say. She grips back of Dolly's chair.*) Do you understand money? Many thousands of dollars? That is the extent to which I care about your medicine. (*She moves to front of stage, facing audience.*) You see, Morris and I have made . . . an arrangement. We've bought the old canning factory back of the depot. We plan to bottle the dropsy cure there.

DOLLY. (*Disbelieving.*) My . . . not my . . . ?

VERENA. (*Spinning round to confront her.*) I won't be crossed, I warn you. (*Then more calmly as she crosses to Dolly's chair.*) This is no childish proposition: I've planned it for a long time. (*Again placing her hands on back of Dolly's chair.*) Morris and I are going to Washington this week to register a patent . . . naming you as the inventor, naturally. Of course we will need the complete formula. Morris, will you write this down . . . ? (*Ritz extracts from his inside suit pocket a pen and pad. He waits like an expectant stenographer.*)

CATHERINE. (*Stepping away from door.*) Don't you do it, Dollyheart. That One and This One—(*Points to Ritz.*) they're nothing but crooks out to steal our dropsy.

VERENA. (*Takes a seething, silent step toward Catherine.*) Get out. (*A second step.*) Out. (*Another step.*) Out. (*Catherine backs through the kitchen door. Pause. Verena looks a long look at Dolly, who is sitting as if she were in a coma.*) We're waiting.

DOLLY. (*Quietly.*) It won't do. Because you haven't any right. You haven't any right, Verena. (*She rises, looks at Ritz with dignity.*) Nor you, sir.

RITZ. (*Putting away pen and pad.*) Maybe—uh . . . ha . . . ha . . . uh . . . another day. (*Stands up.*) Verena . . . uh . . . if you want me I'll be at the hotel.

VERENA. (*Her eyes set hypnotically on Dolly.*) Collin, take Dr. Ritz to the door. (*Collin sulkily obeys her, he and Ritz exit through dining room door* U. R. *We see Ritz come out front door, he walks swiftly across the stage* R. to L.—*midway he stops, snaps his fingers, lifts his eyebrows and exits into the* L. *wings whistling. During this, the scene in the dining room has remained fixed, a tableau: Verena staring at Dolly, Dolly looking at the floor. Then Verena glides toward table.*) These are facts! (*She raps her knuckles on table, she does this at the end of each of the following sentences, accompanying these gestures by moving a step or two nearer Dolly who, in her turn, takes an awkward step backwards, thus they circle around the table, always several feet apart.*) I paid three thousand for that old factory. Have four carpenters working out there at eighty cents an hour. Seven thousand dollars' worth of machinery already ordered. Not to mention what a specialist like Morris Ritz is costing. And why? (*She lets the question echo, then.*) All for you!

DOLLY. (*Sad and failing.*) All for me? (*Then earnestly.*) You are my own flesh, and I love you tenderly; in my heart I love you. I could prove it now by giving you the only thing that has ever been mine: then you would have it all. Please, Sister—(*She falters.*) let this one thing belong to me.

VERENA. (*Bitterly.*) You speak of *giving*. All these years that I've worked like a fieldhand: what haven't I given you? This house, that . . .

DOLLY. You've given everything to me. And to Catherine and to Collin. Except . . . we've earned our way a bit; we've kept a nice home for you, haven't we?

VERENA. (*Laughs and moves to table, glaring around her.*) Oh, a fine home. You and that baboon. (*Motions toward kitchen.*) And that other little scoundrel. (*Stops to look at Dolly directly.*) Has it not struck you that I never ask anyone into this house? And for a very simple reason: I'm *ashamed* to.

DOLLY. (*As though the breath has gone out of her, dropping into chair L. of table.*) I'm sorry. I am truly! I'd always thought there was a place for us here, that you needed us somehow. But it's going to be all right now, Verena. We'll go away.

VERENA. (*Sighing.*) Poor Dolly. (*Picks up a spoon and snuffs R. candle.*) Poor, poor thing. Wherever would you go?

DOLLY. (*After a moment's wait.*) I know a place. (*Verena snuffs L. candle.*)

CURTAIN

(*Black curtain descends to cover painted drop.*)

ACT I

SCENE 2

In the absolute darkness we immediately hear the sound of crowd voices. This is a transition scene that takes place at the front of the stage, before a curtain. A painted drop (like the one shown in photo) may be used for this scene, but it is not necessary. A plain black curtain may be used in its place. The following characters wait down front before the curtain on the blacked-out stage in positions facing the audience for a spotlight to take its turn in picking them out: The Reverend's Wife and The Reverend, The Barber, The Baker's Wife, The Postmaster, The Sheriff. These people will be separately spotlighted for a scene of his own, the crowd voices bridging each appearance. As this scene takes place, the scenery behind the curtain is changed for Act 1, Scene 3.

The Voices fade as the spot falls first on:

REVEREND'S WIFE and THE REVEREND. (*Reverend's Wife is a bull-voiced woman whose steel-rimmed spectacles are too small for her vast and brutal face. She is carrying a market-bag and is dressed for the street—a thin black topcoat and a rather stark little hat. The Reverend, standing somewhat behind his wife, is a small man in a dour too-tight suit. His Wife is, in effect, addressing a friend.*) Edna, you don't know, you don't know, my dear. The Reverend, my husband, and I were with her just now. A heart rending sight . . . wasn't it, Reverend . . . ? (*She looks at her husband, who tries to get out a word of reply, but she booms on, shutting him up.*) Utterly prostrated, she is. No, it's not every day that you find out your only sister is a lunatic. Of course *we* could have told her that lo these many years. Conceive of it . . . ransacking, looting Verena's things right and left and running off in the middle of the night! Not telling a soul. Oh, Edna, what fearful heavy crosses the best of us have to tote. And Verena Talbo, she's among the best of us, we can't deny that. No, there's not a notion in the world where they've got to. (*With freezing*

24

intensity.) I wish I could lay hands on them. . . . (*BLACKOUT.
The crowd voices rise then die down as the spot picks up.*)

BARBER. (*A tiny mincing man, a chatterbox with a shrewd spinsterish voice. His graying hair is parted in the middle. He is wearing a barber's smock, in one hand he has a pair of scissors, in the other a comb, with these he makes a pantomime of giving a haircut.*) Say what you will, Mr. Grump . . . for myself I relish a little excitement. And really this is blissful . . . there hasn't been anything like it since Tubby Twotoes got locked in the iceplant and froze to death. Folks have been swarming in and out of here asking what do I know why Miss Dolly took off to Jesus knows where? I say: at the bottom of the barrel you'll find that fellow calls himself Dr. Ritz. Mr. Grump, you ought to thank your stars you're not in my trade . . . this Dr. Ritz was here for a trim and afterwards I *scalded* my hands trying to sterilize them: his scalp was that much of a scandal. So the way I figure it . . . him and Verena were up to some nefariousness that Miss Dolly found out about and even she couldn't stomach. I say good for her: nothing would tickle me more than to see Verena Talbo get her comeuppance. A little tonic, Mr. Grump? (*BLACKOUT. Voices. The spot shifts to:*)

BAKER'S WIFE. (*An ample woman with a good-natured manner, in short a person anyone ought to like. She is wearing a sweater and a very long apron. Her hair looks as though she had mopped it around in a flour barrel, there is flour on her face and hands. She is speaking to an imaginary customer.*) No, Mrs. Amory—there's not a fresh roll in the place. I burned them all up. I might as well close down the bakery . . . burned up everything all morning. I can't keep my mind on anything . . . what with this worrisome news about Miss Dolly Talbo. It worries me sick to think about her and old Catherine running off from home and creating a scandal like they have. A bit peculiar they may be, Mrs. Amory, but they're as good women as you'll find. Only in a little town like this, prominent citizens have to behave themselves. If they don't, the whole place goes crazy. . . . Sakes, just smell it! There go all my gingerbreads! (*BLACKOUT. Voices. The spot shifts to:*)

POSTMASTER. (*As is the custom in many rural towns, this postmaster, an elderly dry-voiced fellow, doubles as the telegraph agent. He is coatless: his striped shirt has a starched, very high*

white collar. He is wearing green sleeve-supporters and a green eyeshade, in his hand he holds a batch of telegrams. He has a habit of rocking from one foot to the other. He is talking, we presume to a friend.) Took in quite a haul this morning, Fred. Sent off fifty copies of a fifty-nine word telegram. (*Poring through sheaf of telegrams.*) About Miss Dolly Talbo: her . . . uh . . . disappearance. (*Finding the particular telegram.*) Fred, don't say I said this, but it says: (*Reading.*) "Be on the lookout for following persons believed travelling together. Dolly Augusta Talbo, white, aged fifty, brown hair, not likely to be dangerous, post description bakeries as she is cake eater. Catherine Creek, Negro, pretends to be Indian, age about fifty, strong, likely to be dangerous. Collin Talbo, age fifteen, bad posture, surly natured. All three wanted as runaways!" (*Shuffling telegrams together again.*) With the fifty copies, that cost Verena Talbo over a hundred dollars. I don't doubt she's took to her bed. (*BLACKOUT. Voices. Spot to:*)
SHERIFF. (*A youngish man, squat, powerful, a bully with a rabble-rousing voice. He is wearing a leather jumper to which there is pinned a silver Sheriff's star, he has on riding breeches and laced-up boots and sports a pistol in a hip-holster. He is haranguing what we must believe to be a large group of men.*) Boys . . . now, boys, as sworn-in deputies, you-all raise your arms and swear to do your duty. (*Lifting his arm.*) Say: I swear to do my duty. (*Offstage male voices echo him, he lowers his arm.*) Your duty is . . . is to find these damn fools. We've got a warrant (*Slaps his pocket.*) on grounds that they plundered and stole property belonging to Miss Verena. What I'm driving at is . . . is we ain't dealing with no ordinary missing persons. What we got is . . . is a case of *crime*. Now, boys, they can't have got far; was only one train through here last night . . . and it didn't stop. (*Pointing with his thumb.*) Brophy, Big Eddie, Sam, you there, you get your flashlight and have a look down all the old water wells . . . you never know where you might find fools like them! (*BLACKOUT. The voices come up fast, a more sombre whispering excitement achieved. The lights come on revealing the five characters in poses suggesting listening on telephones.*)
REVEREND'S WIFE. (*Breathlessly speaking into a make-believe telephone.*) Hello, Edna. . . . I was so afraid you weren't going to answer because . . . listen. Edna, they've found them. Well, not exactly found them. But old Mr. Vanevery over at the grave-

26

yard, he saw them around dawn this morning . . . he said they were headed *into the woods!*

BARBER. (*Into imaginary phone.*) . . . *into the woods?* But *which* woods?

BAKER'S WIFE. (*Into imaginary phone.*) River Woods, you say?

POSTMASTER. (*Into imaginary phone.*) All I've got to say is, they ain't found them yet. River Woods is a big place.

SHERIFF. River Woods, boys! Everybody together and into the woods! (*Voices join in a shout on the last word and cut with the blackout.*)

BLACKOUT

ACT I

SCENE 3

As curtain slowly rises the music changes into a strange and shimmering song, a sound of grass and wind, leaves, voices. The scene is midmorning in an autumn wood, and the stage is dominated by a luxurious tree with thick surface roots and a gnarled, very foreshortened trunk. On either side of the tree its branches extend almost the width of the stage—the effect should be more airy than dense: its leaves, rust and speckled, green and greenish-gold, are shivering in a wind, rippling like the colors on a peacock's tail. In the lower center of this tree there is a tree-house, a sturdy raft that must suitably accommodate four persons: it is fully exposed to view, and, because the trunk of the tree is in trick perspective, will seem rather higher up than actually it can be. At the right of the stage we see the beginning edge of a field of tall straw-blonde grass. A painted back-drop, looming behind the tree, and curving into the flies, suggests sky and birds, the depths of a forest, at night it will shine with a sprinkling of stars. There are plants and falling vines of ivy, and front-stage, at the L., there is a small moss-colored mound scattered over with leaves. Front stage, R., there is a rock suggesting an open-air fireplace, with some sticks nearby.

27

Dolly and Collin are seated in the tree-house, surrounded by a collection of cardboard boxes, L. and R., a barrel C., and cloth sacks. Some eggs, an empty jelly jar, two bottles of wine and four tin cups are also in the tree-house. Dolly is wearing a long-skirted suit of gray and durable material, around her shoulders there is a dainty sealskin tippet, and she is wearing a hat, a bonnet really, decorated with what was known in other days as a "traveling veil." She is in a listening attitude, her feet dangling over the edge of the tree-house. Collin is sitting at her L., with his legs crossed Indian-fashion. He is wearing tan trousers, a blue sweater, a tan muffler. For some while after the curtain has gone up we may hear the music, and it is as though its theme has set the scene in motion, the grass trembles, the leaves sway, paper butterflies, suspended from the flies by silk threads, swirl and flutter. Gradually the music is like a call that has almost ceased to echo. A certain stillness settles.

DOLLY. Do you hear? That is the grass harp.

COLLIN. (*With a searching glance.*) Where?

DOLLY. Oh, not anywhere. The wind. There in the great field of grass. (*A whispery rush of music, then.*) A harp of voices . . . telling a story. It knows the stories of everyone: and when we are dead it will tell ours, too.

COLLIN. If the story was about me . . . (*Pause, then.*) What would it say?

DOLLY. It would say . . . it would say what you did when you lived. I've often heard my Papa. When we were girls he used to stomp around on cold mornings and sing songs while he built the fires. I've heard the grass telling about those cold mornings. (*Catherine enters from L. up stage. She is very dressed up in a navy blue cloth coat and a black straw hat decorated with celluloid cherries. She is carrying the goldfish bowl which is filled with water and the fish.*)

CATHERINE. (*Singing as she enters.*)
Sister Mary wore, Sister Mary wore three lengths of chain,
Ev'ry link was Jesus' name!
I ain't gonna grieve, gonna grieve my Lord,
Ain't gonna grieve, gonna grieve my Lord,

Ain't gonna grieve, gonna grieve my Lord, my Lord no more.
Oh, the tallest tree in Paradise,
Christians calls it The Tree of Life,
I ain't gonna grieve, gonna grieve my Lord,
Ain't gonna grieve, gonna grieve my Lord,
Ain't gonna grieve, gonna grieve my Lord, my Lord no more.

COLLIN. (*To Catherine.*) Where was you so long?

CATHERINE. (*Holding goldfish bowl up to the light and scrutinizing it.*) One thing I was doing, I was down to the river freshening the water in Buster's bowl. He can't breathe in no dirty water. Give me a hand, sugar, help us up. (*There are easy footholds in the treetrunk and strong trailing vines to grip.*) Gonna fall, gonna bust our heads . . . don't I know it!

COLLIN. I don't see why the hell you wanted to bring that fish with you anyway.

CATHERINE. (*Settling herself on top of a box that is between, and a little behind, Collin and Dolly. Fishbowl is held in her lap and she idly stirs the water with her finger.*) Least he don't sass me like some. Just now, down to the river, the current was so strong and Buster got swept right out of the bowl. He could have swam way away. All I did was whistle to him (*She whistles.*) and he come straight back into here. (*She taps bowl.*) He don't leave me and I don't leave him. (*Suddenly to Dolly.*) What's ailing you, Dollyheart? You hearing dead folks again? (*A breeze rustles the leaves, the grass, we hear the whistlings of a whippoorwill, a mocking bird.*) Every time this time of year you start hearing dead folks. But, sugar, that's only the grass has gone dry now and the wind makes it sound funny.

DOLLY. But the wind is us. (*Leaning her head on Catherine's knee.*) It gathers and remembers all our voices, then sends them talking and telling through the leaves and the fields. . . . I've heard Papa clear as day.

CATHERINE. All I wish, I wish a powerful big breeze would blow all that foolishness out of your head and set you to studying our predicament. We are homeless people with few assets. Exactly, now, what are our assets? (*Dolly extracts a man's wallet from her pocket and makes a muttering count of dollars and small silver.*)

COLLIN. Biddy Skinner owes me five bucks . . . maybe I should walk into town and get it from him.

CATHERINE. Uh uh. You'd just take that money and scoot off to the poolhall. Besides which, we can't none of us separate.

DOLLY. (*Completing her tabulations.*) . . . twenty-five and ten makes thirty-five. We've got forty-three dollars and thirty-five cents. And my cameo.

CATHERINE. I know somebody rode a bus the whole way to Mexico City, Mexico . . . for fifteen dollars.

DOLLY. That's nice, dear. But we can't go to Mexico. We don't speak the language. And it's a very dry sort of place. No rivers and forests; and without a forest, how could we make the dropsy cure? I think we ought to stay right here.

COLLIN. (*Reluctantly, as he lights a cigarette.*) . . . But we can't.

CATHERINE. You recall how we read in the paper where a man bought a castle across the ocean and brought it every bit home with him? If he could do that . . . what's to keep us from loading some rooms of our house on a wagon and hauling them down here?

DOLLY. Nothing. Except that it's *not* our house. It belongs to Verena.

CATHERINE. You wrong, sugar. If you feed a man, and wash his clothes, and born his children you and that man are married, that man is yours. If you sweep a house, and tend its fires and fill its stove, and there is love in you all the years you are doing this, then you and that house are married, that house is yours. The way I see it, the house up there belongs to *us,* in the eyes of God, we could put That One right out.

DOLLY. Yes, but . . .

COLLIN. (*Rising, leaning his hand against an upper branch.*) Maybe I'll go over to Pensacola and join the navy. I could join the navy and send you my pay check.

CATHERINE. (*Scornfully.*) I'll bet you'd send it, too!

COLLIN. Sure I would. You'd be my dependents.

DOLLY. No, no. Always wondering where you were . . . I would feel so old.

CATHERINE. Not that I'm against you contributing to our support . . . with a steady honest job.

COLLIN. (*Peevishly.*) I'm hungry.

CATHERINE. Well, there's plenty to eat. (*Puts fishbowl down beside her, then starts rummaging in a box.*) We won't starve a while yet. I stripped the pantry . . . didn't leave a biscuit for That One's breakfast. (*Begins passing food out of box, apples, oranges, cupcakes. Suddenly, like a cracking whip, we hear a distant-sounding rifle shot. Silence, a lonely crying of birds, the occupants of the tree-house sit galvanized—as one, their heads turn and they gaze expectantly at someone the audience cannot yet see. It is Judge Charlie Cool who, staring up into the foliage and the sky, enters at L., walking backwards. He is carrying a rifle, a batch of dead squirrels, attached to his trouser belt, swings against his hip. The trousers are faded khaki, he is wearing a sharkskin windbreaker, army shoes, and an old yellowed corduroy hunting cap. He is a retired county circuit judge of sixty, youthful looking and with a modest and countrified manner. As he approaches, the three in the tree seem to hold their breath: Dolly lowers veiling of her hat, as if to camouflage herself, Collin squats on his haunches, Catherine, her hands over her face, peeks between spread fingers. Judge reaches far R. front of stage and pauses, he aims his rifle, pointing it toward the audience, then gradually swings barrel around until his aim is within inches of the tree-house.*) Judge Charlie Cool! Don't you dare shoot us!

DOLLY. (*Timidly.*) Please . . . I'd be obliged if you wouldn't.

JUDGE. (*Lowering rifle and letting out a startled hearty laugh that ends on a puzzled note.*) Well, good day. Good day, Catherine Creek, Collin boy. (*Lifting off his cap.*) Is that you, Miss Dolly?

DOLLY. (*With dignity.*) It is.

JUDGE. What happened . . . a wildcat chase you?

CATHERINE. Wildcats! Where you see any wildcats?

DOLLY. The Judge is only spoofing. (*Doubtfully.*) Aren't you?

JUDGE. No, ma'am. I've tracked several big cats in these very woods. 'Course they won't be bothering you . . . they don't come out till night. (*Catherine and Dolly exchange serious glances.*) But, Miss Dolly, say now, what are you folks doing up there?

DOLLY. (*After a thoughtful moment.*) Sitting.

JUDGE. I can see that, but uh . . .

DOLLY. (*As though to change the subject.*) A fine mess of squirrels you've got there, Judge.

JUDGE. (*Detaching squirrels from his belt.*) Take a couple They're real tender if you fry them in deep fat. (*Leaning rifle*

32

against the tree trunk.) Wait a minute. I'll bring them up to you.
DOLLY. (*Alarmed.*) You needn't do that. Just leave them on the ground.
JUDGE. (*Hoisting himself up into the tree.*) Better not. Ants will get at them. (*Everyone shifts to make more room for Judge, and Collin, climbing a little higher into the tree, straddles a branch above their heads and sits there munching an apple. Catherine moves to box L., leaving barrel C. for Judge. Pounding his foot on the boards.*) A tree-house. And a dagderned good one.
CATHERINE. Won't be if you don't quit that stomping.
DOLLY. Won't you sit down, Judge, and join us in a small repast?
JUDGE. I can't say I mind as I do. That's kind of you. My daughter-in-law, she doesn't set much of a table . . . she doesn't believe in breakfast at all. (*Seating himself.*) Not like my wife: Irene came from hardy stock, she understood a man ought to eat . . . long as she lived I never went without an adequate breakfast: pork chops and mashed potatoes and squirrels and possum . . .
DOLLY. (*She and Catherine have been exploring food packages together.*) May I offer you a drumstick?
JUDGE. Thank you, ma'am. (*After biting into drumstick, and as he chews.*) Reason I didn't know it was you a while ago, Miss Dolly . . . I couldn't see you for all that veil.
DOLLY. (*Raising and pinning back veil.*) I believe it's customary for ladies to wear a veil when they go travelling. We intend to travel . . . eventually.
JUDGE. Don't.
DOLLY. What . . . wear a veil?
JUDGE. Travel.
DOLLY. Oh, it's not that we want to. None of us are travellers . . . we've never been anywhere. Except once on Collin's birthday we went to Birmingham and saw the Ringling Brothers, Barnum and Bailey. I enjoyed the freaks very much.
CATHERINE. One of them freaks, Judge . . . you bear a resemblance to him. In the face. The rest of him was all feathers He went quack quack quack.
COLLIN. It was a fake.
CATHERINE. Was not!
COLLIN. Was so.
CATHERINE. You said every one of them was a fake . . . 'cause you were jealous. Jealous of them freaks 'cause they were so un-

usual and the center of attention. (*Staring at Judge.*) . . . a striking resemblance.

DOLLY. (*Nibbling a cupcake.*) Anyway . . . that's the only time we ever went anywhere.

JUDGE. You have a good home, all of you. Stay in it.

DOLLY. (*Despairingly.*) Yes.

CATHERINE. Tell the Judge the truth. How That One and the little rat was stealing the dropsy . . .

DOLLY. Hush. Now hush. I mean it.

JUDGE. (*With soft-spoken concern.*) Are you in trouble, Miss Dolly?

CATHERINE. Trouble! Don't let me *commence!*

DOLLY. (*To Catherine, icily.*) Have you no particle of pride?

CATHERINE. Who are you? My Dollyheart, or some kind of hypocrite? The Judge, he's a friend, he ought to know how after a lifetime of toil we were shown the door of our own house.

DOLLY. For one thing, we weren't shown the door. We left. (*With lowered eyes.*) I can't bear talk against my sister. She's worked hard, she deserves to have things as she wants them. It's our fault, some way we failed her. . . . (*Shuddering, beginning to cry gently. Catherine moves to her.*) There was no place for us in her house.

JUDGE. Don't weep. Don't weep, Miss Dolly.

CATHERINE. (*Using lifted hem of her skirt to dry Dolly's eyes.*) All them tears . . . they'll stain our pretty clothes. . . .

JUDGE. It may be there is no place for any of us. Except we know there is, somewhere; and if we found it, but lived there only a moment, we could count ourselves blessed. This could be your place. (*Looking up into tree.*) And mine.

CATHERINE. (*As she finishes drying Dolly's eyes.*) You can have my share. You surely can. Judge, please, sir, lend me one of them cigarettes.

DOLLY. (*In a voice still choked and tearful.*) Catherine! I've never known you to touch tobacco.

CATHERINE. It must be a comfort, so many folks speak in its favor. (*Judge strikes match for her cigarette.*) And, Dollyheart, when you get to be our age you've got to look for comforts. (*She puffs amateurishly at cigarette the Judge has lighted for her. Judge sits on box L.*)

DOLLY. (*Intensely curious.*) What is it like?

CATHERINE. Delicious. Want a taste?

COLLIN. (*Suddenly alert and listening.*) Shh! Shh! (*The leaves rustle, there is a perceptible darkening of light. Those entering from L. are: Reverend, Reverend's Wife, Choir Mistress, and a rolypoly man called Big Eddie Stover. Those entering from R. are: Sheriff, accompanied by two men, one called Brophy, the other Sam. They do not come in as a group, but appear separately or in stealthy pairs. Reverend is a scrawny man, smaller than his wife, and he is wearing a black suit and a black fedora. His Wife and the Choir Mistress, a thin severe woman with an odd baby-talk voice contradictory to her appearance, cautiously walk hand in hand. It is Choir Mistress who first sees the congregation in the tree. She nudges Reverend's Wife and stares raptly up at the tree-house, then, in unison, they take a step backward and scream.*)

SHERIFF. (*Hand on his hip-holster.*) All right now, come down from there, the lot of you!

REVEREND'S WIFE. (*To Sheriff.*) We agreed to let the Reverend tend to this . . . in the merciful manner of the Lord's name. (*Judge laughs, she gives him a withering look.*) You've lost your mind, have you, Charlie Cool? What are you doing with these people in the first place?

JUDGE. (*Rocking as though he were in a rocking chair.*) Just a-sittin' and a-talkin'. Any objection?

REVEREND'S WIFE. Shame! For shame!

CHOIR MISTRESS. (*Baby lisping.*) Shame! For shame!

REVEREND. (*With an air of getting in a word edgewise.*) I speak to you on behalf of your sister, that gracious good woman . . .

REVEREND'S WIFE and CHOIR MISTRESS. (*Together.*) That she is!

REVEREND. —who has this day received a lamentable shock.

REVEREND'S WIFE and CHOIR MISTRESS. (*Together.*) That she has!

REVEREND. How can you come so far from God as to sit up in a tree like a drunken Indian?

CATHERINE. (*Flat-voiced.*) I resent that.

DOLLY. (*Casually dusting her skirt.*) Consider a moment, Reverend, and you will realize that we are nearer God than you . . . by several yards.

35

JUDGE. (*Chuckling appreciatively.*) Good for you, Miss Dolly. I call that a good answer.

REVEREND'S WIFE. I'd thought you were a Christian, Judge Cool. My ideas of a Christian do not include laughing at and encouraging a poor mad woman.

JUDGE. Mind whom you name as mad, dear lady. That isn't especially Christian, either.

REVEREND'S WIFE. (*Defensively.*) It's a fact . . . she is . . . she's a lunatic.

CATHERINE. Hold on. Hold on, preacher lady. One more word, I'll come down there and slap you bowlegged.

REVEREND'S WIFE. (*Turning and moving to others, gasping, stunned.*) Every one of you: you're witnesses! You heard what she said, that black . . . black (*Catherine, pushing back her sleeves, starts to step off raft—Dolly and Judge restrain her.*)

REVEREND. Answer me this, Charlie Cool. We are here to do the Lord's will . . .

CHOIR MISTRESS. (*Lisping.*) In a spirit of mercy.

REVEREND. —are you a disbeliever in the Lord's will?

JUDGE. (*Amused.*) The Lord's will? You don't know what that is any more than I do. For myself, I think the Lord must be very satisfied to see us sheltered in one of His trees.

SHERIFF. (*Advancing, ready for action.*) To hell with all that!

REVEREND'S WIFE. (*To Sheriff.*) Under no circumstances will we tolerate swearing. Will we, Reverend?

SHERIFF. (*Turning on Reverend.*) I'm in charge here. This is a matter for the law.

JUDGE. (*Quietly.*) Whose law, Sheriff? Remember that I sat in the court-house twenty-four years. Take care. You have no legal right whatever to interfere with Miss Dolly.

SHERIFF. (*In coaxing, wheedling tones.*) Miss Dolly, you've always been a peaceable person. Come down . . . (*With a foothold in the tree trunk and extending his hand as if to help Dolly.*) come home: you don't want to miss your dinner.

DOLLY. We've eaten, thank you. Have you? There's another drumstick if you'd like it.

SHERIFF. (*Climbing determinedly toward her.*) You make it hard on me, ma'am.

JUDGE. All right, Sheriff. You lay a hand on any one of us . . . (*Raises his foot.*) I'll kick you in the head. (*Sheriff keeps climbing*

36

toward tree-house, and Judge kicks at him—whereupon, amid much hollering, the following things happen: Sheriff catches Judge's foot and starts to pull. Big Eddie Stover pulls at Sheriff, and Brophy and Sam join this tug-of-war chain—with Reverend struggling at the end. Catherine holds onto Judge and prevents his being pulled out of tree-house, then Collin coming down from his higher perch, takes over this job, and Catherine fetches her fish bowl, with a hand carefully applied to the rim to keep fish from spilling out, she begins to pour water onto Sheriff's head. Throughout this Dolly has sat with a squeezed-up face and with her fingers in her ears. Then suddenly Judge's boot comes off in Sheriff's hand, Sheriff, his three deputies and Reverend all crash back on one another and collapse on the ground. Reverend's Wife and Choir Mistress, augmenting the disaster, kneel beside the fallen men with whining cries of distress.)

REVEREND'S WIFE. (Trying to lift Reverend.) Speak to me! Speak! Are you dead, lover? (Collin and Judge descend from tree-house. Judge stands and hops on one foot so that his shoeless foot does not touch ground.)

JUDGE. (To Sheriff, who is picking himself up.) I'll thank you for my boot.

SHERIFF. (Viciously throwing shoe at Judge.) If you weren't so old, I'd damn well knock you down.

JUDGE. I'm not so old, Sheriff: just old enough to think men ought not to settle their differences in front of ladies. On the other hand, I'm ready if you are.

SHERIFF. (After spitting between forked fingers.) Hell, I'm not not going to take the blame for hitting an old guy.

JUDGE. Or the credit for standing up to one, either. Go on, tuck your shirt in your pants and trot along home.

SHERIFF. (Appealing to Dolly and Catherine in the tree.) Save yourselves a lot of trouble: get out of there and come along with me now. (Neither Catherine nor Dolly stirs, although Dolly drops her veil, as though lowering a curtain on the subject once and for all.)

REVEREND'S WIFE. (Portentously.) Never mind, Sheriff. They've had their chance. (She starts to exit L., Sheriff, her husband and others going ahead of her. Then, just before she goes offstage, Reverend's wife turns round.) You may think you are getting away with something. But let me tell you there will be a retribution—not in heaven, right smack here on earth! (*She exits* L.)

CHOIR MISTRESS. Right smack here on earth! (*She follows Reverend's Wife. Then, as the stage dims to a silvery twilight, a curtain of music falls, and a transitional time lapse, in the most stylized sense, occurs before our eyes. Dolly and Catherine climb down out of the tree, Catherine carrying a bundle of two scrap-quilts. She spreads quilts on ground over the exposed roots of the tree. We see Judge and Collin gathering sticks and twigs for a fire which they build—without "lighting" it—in front of where quilts have been spread. Collin brings barrel, box and sack down from tree-house and sets them around fireplace for others to sit on. The sack is in* C. *of fireplace area, the barrel at* R. *and the box at* L. *of fireplace area. The music fades, like a last sigh of wind—for a moment the silence sings with twilight sounds, the shrilling of cicadas, bleating of frogs, the mournful wail of whippoorwills.*)

DOLLY. (*Standing by tree trunk and leaning a little against it.*) You were very brave, Judge.

JUDGE. (*Adding sticks to fire.*) No. I was afraid. I'm always afraid of righteous people. . . .

DOLLY. However that may be, you are a brave man. (*As if to herself.*) All of them behaving ugly that way, acting mad enough to kill us. Though I can't see why, or what it has to do with Verena: she knew we were going away to leave her in peace. I told her. (*Gazing around at twilight.*) But it's getting dark . . . you should be starting home.

JUDGE. Two women and a boy? With night coming on? And the Sheriff, those fools, up to God knows what? I'm sticking with you. (*He sits on sack in* C. *of fireplace area.*)

CATHERINE. (*She is sitting on barrel at* R. *end of fireplace, she spreads her hands in front of fire.*) That feels mighty good . . . only what we need is a sip of blackberry wine. Collin sugar, hop up there—(*She means for him to go to tree-house and bring down wine.*) I brought along two bottles case anybody was feeling the cold. I'm feeling it. (*Collin climbs up into tree.*)

DOLLY. (*Coming to fire, holding her hands over it.*) But won't they be worried, Judge? Your family, I mean.

JUDGE. (*Soberly.*) They won't be missing me. We're not . . . close that way. (*Breaking in half some sticks and piling them on fire.*) I'm more like a roomer. They let me have my room. (*Collin has climbed down from tree and arrived with wine and four tin* cups. *Dolly sits on box at* L. *end of fireplace. Collin, at* R. *of Catherine, pours wine.*)

CATHERINE. (*Passing a cup full of wine to each person.*) Dolly-heart's daddy, old Mr. Talbo, every time he poured hisself a little taste of something, he'd say: Here's winking at the devil. Well . . . (*She raises her cup, others follow suit.*)

COLLIN, CATHERINE, JUDGE. (*Together.*) Here's winking at the . . .

DOLLY. (*Strained and listening.*) Hush. Hush.

COLLIN. (*Looking off to* R.) It's only an owl. A snowy owl.

DOLLY. I keep imagining . . . (*With a certain exhaustion she sinks to the box.*) Do you think they will bother us again?

JUDGE. (*Nodding, and then.*) We must be ready for them. But if we are to defend our position, we must know what it is. We are in trouble . . . because we are troubled. Miss Dolly, how long? Thirty, forty years? It was that far ago that I remember you . . . riding to town in your father's wagon . . . never getting down from the wagon because you didn't want us town children to see you had no shoes.

CATHERINE. (*Nudging Collin.*) What did I tell you? Not a shoe to our name.

JUDGE. (*Continuing to Dolly.*) All the years that I've seen you, never known you, not ever recognized what you are: a spirit, a pagan . . .

DOLLY. (*Mildly alarmed.*) A pagan?

JUDGE. Well . . . a spirit, someone not to be calculated by the eye alone. Spirits are accepters of life, they grant its differences, and consequently are usually on the right side. Myself, I should never have been a judge; as such, I was too often on the wrong side; the law doesn't admit differences. Do you remember old Carper . . . the fisherman who had a houseboat down on the river? He was chased out of town . . . wanted to marry that pretty little colored girl. I think she works for Mrs. Postum now. And you know she loved him, I used to see them when I was fishing, they were very happy together. She was to him what no one has been to me: *the one person in the world* . . . from whom nothing is held back. Still, if he had succeeded in marrying her, it would have been the Sheriff's duty to arrest and my duty to sentence him. I sometimes imagine that many whom I've called guilty

39

have passed the real guilt on to me. It's partly that that makes me want once before I die to be right on the right side.

CATHERINE. You on the right side now . . . if that's all it takes to satisfy you.

DOLLY. (*In a voice that lingers inquiringly.*) The one person in the world . . .

JUDGE. I mean a person to whom everything can be said. Am I an idiot to want such a thing? But oh, the energy we spend hiding from one another, afraid as we are of being identified. But for us there is no longer any need to worry about the picture we present . . . (*Gesturing toward tree-house.*) there we are: four fools with a roost in a tree. The only problem now . . . (*He laughs.*) is to find out who we truly are.

CATHERINE. I know who I am.

JUDGE. By scraps and bits I've in the past surrendered myself to strangers . . . men who got off at the next station: put together, maybe they would have made the one person in the world. But there he is with a dozen different faces moving down a hundred separate streets. This is my chance to find that man . . . you are him, Miss Dolly, Collin, all of you.

CATHERINE. (*To Judge.*) I should have told you. . . . go easy on the wine: it's, uh, *strong*.

DOLLY. (*To Catherine.*) Please . . . if you can't be respectful, then take a nap.

CATHERINE. I'm only saying: I'm no man with a dozen faces. The notion!

DOLLY. But, Judge, I'm not sure I know what it is you have in mind we should tell each other. Secrets?

JUDGE. Secrets, no, no. Speak of the twilight, the fact there are no fireflies. What one says hardly matters—only the trust with which it is said, the sympathy with which it is received. My wife, a remarkable woman, we might have shared anything, and yet, yet . . . (*Bringing tips of his fingers together as if in illustration.*) we could not *touch*. She died in my arms, and at the last I said: Are you happy, Irene? Have I made you happy? Happy, happy, happy, those were her last words: equivocal. I have never understood whether she was saying yes, or merely answering with an echo: I should know if I'd ever known her. (*Then, with difficulty.*) My . . . son. He does not admire me. I've wanted him to,

40

more as a man than as a father. Unfortunately, he and his wife feel they know something shameful about me.

DOLLY. You mustn't tell us if it pains you.

JUDGE. No . . . I'll tell you what it is: what it is they hold against me. Five years ago, nearer six, I sat down in a train-seat where some child had left a child's magazine. I saw on the back cover addresses of children who wanted to correspond with other children. There was a little girl in Alaska. I sent her a picture postcard: Lord, it seemed a harmless and pleasant thing to do. She wrote me back . . . about her father's sheep ranch, and the Northern lights. And she sent a picture of herself . . . a wise and kind-looking child. So I found an old kodak made of myself on a fishing trip when I was fifteen . . . out in the sun and with a trout in my hand. I wrote her as though I were still that boy, told her of the gun I'd got for Christmas, how the dog had had pups and what we'd named them. To be growing up again and have a sweetheart in Alaska . . . well, it was fun for an old man sitting alone listening to the noise of a clock. Two years ago, when I told her I was getting ready for law school, she sent me a gold nugget . . . (*He takes nugget out of his pocket and holds it out for others to see.*) it would bring me good fortune, she said.

DOLLY. And that's what they think is shameful? Because you've helped keep company a lonely little child in Alaska? It snows there so much.

JUDGE. (*Returning nugget to his pocket.*) My son's wife, she found out about the letters. They think it all a sign of . . . (*Taps his head.*)

CATHERINE. (*Extending her wine cup for Collin to refill.*) I had a letter once. Still got it somewhere. Kept it twenty years wondering who wrote it. Said, Hello, Catherine, come on to Birmingham and marry with me, love, Bill.

DOLLY. A *grown* man asked you to marry him . . . and you never told one word of it to me?

CATHERINE. (*Shrugging.*) Well, Dollyheart, what was the Judge saying? You don't tell anybody everything. Besides, I've known a peck of Bills . . . wouldn't study marrying any of them. (*Thoughtfully.*) What worries my mind is, which one of the Bills was it wrote that letter. It could be the Bill that put the roof on the chicken-house; 'course, by the time the roof was up . . . my goodness, I have got old, been a long day since I've given it two

41

thoughts. There was Bill that came to plow the garden, one spring. That man sure could plow a *straight* row . . . went away on a Pullman job: might have been him wrote me that letter. Or Bill . . . uh uh, his name was Fred. (*Smacking her lips.*) This wine is mighty good. (*All four stare into the fire, and we hear rustlings in the leaves, the hooting of an owl.*)

COLLIN. (*Frowning, getting up, moving to C.*) I . . . you're wrong, Judge.

JUDGE. (*Moving to him.*) How so, son?

COLLIN. I'm not in trouble: I'm nothing . . . or would you call that my trouble? They kicked me out of school on account of I was such a troublemaker and couldn't even learn the alphabet; anyway, I never would have got past third grade if I hadn't caught Miss Burkett necking old Tubby Twotoes. So I lie awake thinking what do I know how to do: fool around. And I get scared when I think maybe that's all it will ever come to: fooling around. Another thing is, I'm *mean.* You probably heard the thing I did to Whitey Kuzak: grabbed hold of him and bit off a good hunk of his ear. . . . I said the reason was he insulted me: but pure meanness was why I did it. What I'm saying is, I've got no feelings . . . except for Dolly and I guess Catherine, which is different. I know a lot of girls, I even like one of them a whole lot . . .

CATHERINE. Floozies, that's all he knows.

COLLIN. (*To Catherine.*) Maude Riordan's not one ounce of a floozy, you hear me? (*To Judge.*) It's me . . . you'd be surprised . . . the thoughts in my head. Only with Maude I try not to have these thoughts. The night of the Baptist Church dance I made her one of those flower knick-knacks girls wear here— (*He jiggles his breast.*) made it myself with sweet peas . . . and I took her to a roast beef and mashed-potato dinner at the Philadelphia Café. See, I wanted to be nice and decent . . . but then, after the dance I'm walking her home . . . and it's like somebody was running after us, this other me, the one with the thoughts. And I start running, too . . . 'cause I don't want him to catch up with me: I just left Maude standing there in the road, and ran like hell. (*Pause, then.*) You said before about the one person in the world. Why can't I think of her like that? . . . Then I couldn't have just the thoughts about her that I have about other girls. Maybe, if I could care for somebody that way, I'd make plans and carry them out.

42

JUDGE. Son, I'd say you were going at it the wrong way first. How could you care about one girl? Have you ever cared about one leaf? We are speaking of love. A leaf, a handful of seed . . . begin with these, learn a little what it is to love. First, a leaf, a fall of rain, then someone to receive what a leaf has taught you, what a fall of rain has ripened. No easy process, understand; it could take a lifetime, it has mine, and still I've never mastered it . . . I only know how true it is: that love is a chain of love, as nature is a chain of life.

DOLLY. (*With an intake of breath.*) Then . . . I've been in love all my life. (*More lamely.*) Well, no. (*Rising.*) No, I guess not. I've never loved a . . . a gentleman. You might say that I've never had the opportunity. Except Papa. (*Moving, drifting as in a dream toward the moss-covered mound at the L. of the stage.*) But . . . I have loved everything else. Like the color pink. When I was a child I had one colored crayon, and it was pink: I drew pink cats, pink trees —— And the box I kept, it's somewhere in the attic now, I must ask Verena please to give it to me, it would be nice to see my first loves again. It's only . . . it's only a dried honeycomb, an empty hornet's nest, other things, oh, an orange stuck with cloves and a jaybird's egg. (*Looking at Judge.*) Love is a chain of love. Because . . . when you love one thing, then you can love another, and that is owning, that is something to live with. (*After pause, Dolly moves into a shaft of moonlight stage L.*)

CATHERINE. I've got Buster up there . . . (*Gestures toward tree-house.*) just 'cause I like him don't make me love the world. Love a lot of mess, my foot. You can talk what you want . . . I say people ought to keep more things to themselves. The deep down ownself part of you, that's the good part: what's left of a human being that goes around speaking his privates? (*Lifting one of the quilts and handing it to Judge.*) Judge, take this other quilt and wrap it round you. . . . (*To Dolly, who is standing front-stage looking at sky.*) Man's shivering like was Hallowe'en. (*Rising, and moving to Dolly, Judge drapes quilt around her like a cape. Dolly takes no notice of him coming but continues to stare, in profile, up into the sky. Catherine draws Collin under the wing of her arm.*) Snuggle up, hard-head; you cold like anybody else. (*Collin and Catherine settle down on a quilt as if to go to sleep. The stage now is night-like, moon-lighted; faint stars flicker on back-drop—the whippoorwills' call is clearer, longer.*)

43

DOLLY. (*Still gazing at sky.*) What did you wish?

JUDGE. (*Standing behind Dolly.*) Wish, Miss Dolly?

DOLLY. Didn't you see? (*Pointing.*) There was a shooting star. (*Excitedly, and with her voice trailing as though she were following the shooting path of a star.*) Oh . . . oh . . . look . . . again! I hope you made a wish that time.

JUDGE. Yes . . . I did.

DOLLY. (*Looking at him over her shoulder.*) Tell me.

JUDGE. You first.

DOLLY. (*Looking back at sky.*) I only wished . . . that I could see another one. And you?

JUDGE. My wish . . . Miss Dolly . . . won't you . . . (*Glances round at Catherine and Collin to satisfy himself that they are asleep.*)

DOLLY. What . . . ?

JUDGE. (*Touching Dolly's shoulders.*) Be . . . the one person in the world.

DOLLY. (*In a small voice.*) Could I be?

JUDGE. (*Smiling.*) I think so. But I would want you to decide.

DOLLY. It's what I would like, a life made of my own decisions. Except I've never earned the privilege of making up my own mind. (*On the words "my own mind" Judge bends forward, takes her hand, kisses it, but quickly, in a rather frightened way, she drops her hat veiling over her face. Gently, then, Judge takes the rim of the veil and, as in a stately ceremony, draws it back. They look at one another. Music tenuous, a thread, rises as Judge leans and kisses Dolly's forehead. Slowly the lights fade to darkness.*)

CURTAIN

ACT II

Scene 1

SCENE: *The wood.*
It is early morning of the following day, a time when daybreak mists have still not dispersed. The scene is silent with sleep.
Catherine and Collin are huddled asleep by the darkened fire—Dolly, Judge, these two are in the tree-house, they are still upright, wrapped together in a quilt and they are asleep with Judge's head resting on Dolly's shoulder. Dolly's hat is rather askew and Judge's hair is tangled on his forehead. At far R. of stage, standing at the edge of the grass, really in fact posing there, we see Maude Riordan, a girl of sixteen, slight, wistful, very pretty. She is carrying schoolbooks held together by a strap. On tiptoe, moving quickly and with the quality of a dancer, she approaches the burned-out fire and hovers an undecided moment above the sleeping Collin.

MAUDE. (*Whispering.*) Collin . . . Collin. (*Touches him, and then, as though afraid of having done this, retreats several steps. Collin raises himself, opens his eyes and looks straight ahead, not seeing Maude. Catherine grumbles in her sleep, but does not wake up. Maude, whispering.*) Collin . . . here I am. (*Then Collin sees her, gazes at her as if she were part of some continuing dream. From a sitting position he falls forward on his knees.*)
COLLIN. (*Not whispering, but in a hushed voice.*) Aw, Maude. Aw, honey. (*Collin stands up; he and Maude steal softly to front of stage. Collin reaches and pinches her arm.*)
MAUDE. (*Pained and rubbing the place he has pinched.*) You pinch so hard!
COLLIN. I thought I was dreaming because . . . where did you come from?
MAUDE. (*Pointing* R.) From there . . . from the road and

45

through the grass. I was on my way to school . . . and then I wasn't. I heard you were in the woods.

COLLIN. (*Grinning.*) I'll bet you heard.

MAUDE. (*Moving toward moss-covered mound.*) There are terrible stories going around. Everybody at everybody else's house. Oh, Collin, why did you do it?

COLLIN. I didn't do anything.

MAUDE. You did. At least . . . they're going to put you in jail. All of you. I heard Daddy say so.

COLLIN. He'd like that, wouldn't he?

MAUDE. Well, I wouldn't. I wouldn't like it if they locked you in a jail maybe for years and years. (*With sudden dismay.*) You'd even miss the party! Elizabeth Henderson and I are planning the most wonderful Hallowe'en party . . . (*Sorrowfully.*) real wine punch and everything.

COLLIN. A *party.* Good Jesus Christ!

MAUDE. (*Apologetically.*) But you do . . . think of little things like that. Even in the face of terrible disaster, you can think. Somebody I count on . . . somebody I love . . . won't be able to come to my party. You think of little things.

COLLIN. If you have a little mind.

MAUDE. That's not true. My grandfather was practically a genius. And when our house was burning down, what did he worry about? He worried because he heard the telephone ringing inside and there was nobody could answer it. (*A pause, then as she sits on mound* L.) Would you really have gone away, left town without saying a word to me?

COLLIN. Aw, honey, I was thinking of you. Fact is, I might join the navy.

MAUDE. (*Disappointedly.*) Oh.

COLLIN. You could be my dependent. One of them. I mean, I could send you the bus fare to come see me whenever my ship was in port.

MAUDE. I'm sure Daddy would never permit that. (*With a certain sly hopefulness.*) Not unless we were . . . man and wife. (*There follows a strained silence. Collin, with a screwed-up face, scratches his head; Maude fiddles with strap of her schoolbooks.*) I guess I'd better go. I'm already late at school . . . you know what a fuss Miss Burkett will make. (*Collin, as though deep in thought, walks away from her. Rising, Maude looks wanly after him.)* If I don't see you again . . .

COLLIN. *(Coming back to her, then, putting hands in his pockets, and with a very simple air.)* It's going to be a nice day.

MAUDE. *(Looking round her.)* A lovely day . . . I think.

COLLIN. I know a shallow place where we could go wading back and forth across the river . . . the water's still warm enough. *(She shakes her head, without conviction.)* This one day . . . for just a while: Maude, come with me.

MAUDE. I can't . . . don't . . . Daddy will find out I wasn't in school . . .

COLLIN. *(Intensely.)* This one day. *(Slowly Maude lets her schoolbooks slide to the ground and allows Collin to draw her forward by the hand. As they exit through the rear L. of the stage they pause once, glance apprehensively back at the sleepers and, as Maude laughs a hauntingly airy laughter, disappears with light-hearted lilting steps into the depths of the forest. At the sound of Maude's laughter the lights brighten to a more golden daylight and Catherine sits bolt upright. She does not see their exit, only hears the laughter, and stands up, turns around as though searching for its source.)*

CATHERINE. *(Yelling up into the tree.)* Dollyheart . . . that you laughing? Dollyheart . . . wake up there!

DOLLY. *(Opening her eyes and rubbing her temples.)* Don't scream . . . courtesy is so necessary: especially in the morning.

CATHERINE. *(Ominously.)* I heard laughing.

DOLLY. It must have been me; I had a very funny dream: that we'd all been turned into animals . . . you were a walrus and Collin . . . where *is* Collin?

CATHERINE. *(Gazing round, then stamping the quilt as though he might be hiding in its folds.)* I knowed I was missing something. *(She walks to R. of stage and calls.)* Collin!

DOLLY. *(Judge is still sleeping with his head on her shoulder; she taps his head with her knuckles as if it were a door.)* I hate to disturb you . . . excuse me . . . please, Judge, wake up. *(Judge yawns, stretches himself, gives every indication of having come to life—then collapses again, sound asleep with his head nuzzling Dolly's shoulder. She shakes him severely.)* No, no, you mustn't . . . do wake up. *(Judge gradually pulls himself to-*

47

gether. While Dolly has been rousing Judge, Catherine has gone from R. of the stage to L. and, as in the first instance, calls.)

CATHERINE. Collin! (When she wanders toward front of the stage, her eyes hunting the ground as if for a clue to his whereabouts. She sees Maude's schoolbooks, loosens the strap, takes one out, and, facing audience, opens it—her eyes narrow, her teeth clench.) Maude Riordan.

DOLLY. (To Catherine.) What is it? (Begins to descend from tree, Judge following after her.) What have you found?

CATHERINE. (Still facing audience.) Maude Riordan. (Then handing book to Dolly.) There it is . . . her name, wrote down for all to see.

DOLLY. (Taking book and reading from inside cover.) Maude Riordan, eleven Cicada Lane . . .

CATHERINE. She done come here, sneaked here behind our backs and lured him with her wiles . . . though I don't know why a man would give her the time of day; so scrawny . . . nothing on her to pinch.

JUDGE. (Teasing Catherine.) Oh, now . . . I wouldn't go as far as that.

CATHERINE. The floozy. Taking advantage of a boy's innocence to make him leave his loved ones. If they've eloped, I, for one, will never receive her.

JUDGE. (In reply to Dolly, who has turned to him with a distressed expression.) It isn't that serious. I expect I know where they are. (Again in reply to an expression of Dolly's, a questioning one.) After all, I've been Collin's age . . . and know the places in these woods where you might entertain a young lady.

CATHERINE. Then get out there and get them. Cut yourself a switch on the way.

JUDGE. (After a few reluctant steps.) Will you feel safe, Miss Dolly? I don't like it, leaving you alone.

CATHERINE. Nobody's alone. Dolly and us has always made out.

DOLLY. We'll have a pot of coffee ready for you when you come back.

JUDGE. (Walking backwards toward L. rear of stage exit we have seen Maude and Collin take.) When I call like this . . . (He yodels.) you holler back; we'll keep in touch that way, and if I don't hear you I'll come on the run. (Catherine and Dolly watch his exit rear L. Dolly continues to look in the direction in

48

which he has gone, but Catherine takes a seat on moss-covered mound facing audience.)

CATHERINE. *(Resentfully.)* I saw you snuggling him. *(Dolly looks at Catherine with a puzzled air.)* I wake up, first thing I witness: him smooched up to you like a little calf at his mama's titty.

DOLLY. *(With a light, yet embarrassed laugh.)* It was cold, we were cold . . . goodness, I never thought . . .

CATHERINE. *Somebody* was thinking . . . I don't say it was you. *(Dolly sits down at Catherine's feet, she still has Maude's book in her hand.)* Not proper; that's what it's not.

DOLLY. Oh, it's proper. At least . . . Catherine dear, please don't glare at me . . . because if it's not going to make you unhappy, I want to tell you something. *(After pause, during which she stares at book.)* Last night, the Judge . . . well, he proposed.

CATHERINE. *(She sits with an expression of perfect blankness for as long as it takes to count five, then, dead-faced.)* Proposed what?

DOLLY. *(At first surprised, then thoughtful.)* I'm not altogether sure . . . now that I think of it. It seemed to me he meant . . . of course he didn't really say it . . . marriage.

CATHERINE. *(She crosses her legs, as though it is a stunned reflex action, then breaks suddenly into laughter that lasts until she has to wipe her eyes, gasping.)* Tell me . . . tell me every word what transpired.

DOLLY. *(Crossly.)* No, I won't. *(Ruffling through the page of the book, vaguely pretending to read.)* Not if you are going to laugh. I wouldn't anyway.

CATHERINE. *(She rises and, staring down at her, walks round to other side of Dolly.)* Look at me . . . Dollyheart, is you sincere? *(Offstage L., from what must sound like rather a distance, we hear Judge's yodel.)*

DOLLY. *(Anxiously.)* You'd better answer him.

CATHERINE. *(Folding her arms and moving away to C.)* Not me. I'm not speaking to him.

DOLLY. Please . . . he'll think something is wrong.

CATHERINE. Do it yourself. *(Judge calls a second time, and Dolly, standing up, attempts to answer him, she can't make the sound and turns to Catherine with a helpless gesture. With a gesture of exasperation Catherine finally answers Judge herself with a*

49

yodel—indeed, blasts him in a voice strong enough to fell trees.)
. . . Devil take him! I ought to have knowed, him and all that
love-talk: *leaves* . . . love a leaf, my foot.
DOLLY. *(She has approached Catherine, and on the words "love
a leaf" lays her hand on Catherine's wrist.)* You are angry. It
isn't just put-on, is it?
CATHERINE. *(As though she has been touched, and in a gruff
yet gentle tone.)* When you told me that . . . felt like you was
going ahead of me, a different Dolly, all grown-up and different.
And I couldn't follow you, I had to stay where I am; the same
old me. *(Pause; then, with lowered eyes.)* But, Dollyheart, would
you . . . ?
DOLLY. *(Embraces Catherine, then moving a little away.)* He
never really asked me. And if he had, I couldn't really answer. I
guess I've never been required to make up my own mind: either
you or Verena has always done that for me. But until I can . . .
I will never know what is right. *(At this moment we become aware
of Miss Baby Love Dallas. She has entered from R. rear stage and
when we first see her she is mysteriously peering through a foliage
of vine leaves.)*
MISS BABY LOVE. *(First a shrill giggle, then.)* Anyone to home?
*(Then she trips, so to say, into sight—a small creature full of
bounce and strange good spirits. She is teetering on high heels and
is dressed, on the whole, like a dance-hall hostess—there is a very
dubious fur piece slung over her shoulder and she is carrying a
red suitcase pasted with golden stars and pictures of Clara Bow,
Jean Harlow, etc., painted in silver lettering on either side of the
suitcase is the legend SWEETHEART COSMETICS. Swinging this
suitcase, she skips up to Dolly and Catherine.)* I'm Miss Baby
Love Dallas . . . *(As she puts down suitcase.)* three times voted
Sweetest of the Sweethearts travelling for Sweetheart Cosmetics.
(Squinting at Dolly.) You can use everything I've got. *(Then
looking at Catherine, too.)* Both of you. *(Picking up suitcase.)* If
you'll just show me in the house . . .
DOLLY. There isn't any . . . real house.
MISS BABY LOVE. *(She snatches up her suitcase; then, with a
hard and knowing look.)* What are you . . . hoboes? *(Glancing
sharply around, then suddenly giggling.)* Of course . . . it's a
picnic! *(As she sails toward moss-covered mound, there to deposit
her suitcase.)* Am I not a stupid wench? I didn't think you looked

50

like hoboes. Only in my line of endeavor you can well imagine the escapes I've suffered: rape . . . and all that kind of thing. But, oh, the compensations are joyous . . . to bring beauty to the world. It's my duty: I park my little car on country roads and hunt through these backwoods for lonely houses where some poor hag is pining away for beauty. (*She pops open her suitcase and stretches her arms out to Dolly, and, sort of dancing her way toward her, sings. She takes Dolly by the elbow and starts to push her toward the moss-mound—saying to Catherine.*) Come stand over here and watch the miraculous change I'm going to work on Madam.

DOLLY. (*Protesting as Miss Baby Love forces her to sit down on mound.*) Please . . . I beg your pardon . . . don't . . . I don't wear cosmetics . . . Miss—uh—Sweetheart . . .

MISS BABY LOVE. Miss Baby Love Dallas is the name. You have heard of the city of Dallas, Texas? It was founded by terribly close relatives of mine. (*Miss Baby Love, grabbing a large rhinestone-studded mirror out of her suitcase, sternly thrusts it in front of Dolly's face, then, in a deep, threatening voice.*) Look at yourself! (*Dolly meekly does as she is told—then Miss Baby Love whirls round and holds mirror up to Catherine.*) You, too! (*Catherine lolls out her tongue, as though hunting evidence of illness. Miss Baby Love, with a shudder of disgust, promptly whips mirror away, then, wagging a finger.*) But we mustn't give up hope! (*Running a finger along her eyebrow.*) I can beautify anything. (*She looks at herself in mirror and with a sound of disgust replaces mirror in case. She pulls a perfume atomizer out of suitcase and sprays it at them.*) Scotland Fling . . . the odor of heather . . . direct from Paree, France . . . an exclusive with Sweetheart Products . . . fifty cents a pint . . . (*On words "fifty cents a pint" we hear, offstage, a familiar sound: Ritz—whistling. From R., and through the grass, he enters with a supremely confident strut. He is dressed as in Act One, and is wearing an overcoat. Miss Baby Love delightedly eyeing Ritz's entrance.*) Oh, look yonder! . . . A man. (*Squirting Ritz with atomizer as he passes her going toward others, giggling.*) Cute thing. . . .

RITZ. (*Acknowledging Catherine and Dolly, who have received him with hostile silence, tips his hat.*) Good morning, Mademoiselles. I can see the country air agrees with you. (*Striking his*

chest, and with a swift leer at *Miss Baby Love*.) Wish I had time
to store up some in the old . . . pardon the word . . . bosom.
(*Miss Baby Love giggles, takes atomizer to the case.*) But the fact
is . . . (*Glancing over his shoulder.*) I'm in a bit of a dash.

CATHERINE. (*With a gesture.*) Dash on. Nobody here's keeping
you. (*To Dolly.*) Want I should give the Judge a holler? (*Dolly
starts to rise, as though to confront Ritz . . . but Miss Baby
Love, who has once again been rummaging in her suitcase, this
time for a hairy powder puff, forces her to sit down again.*)

MISS BABY LOVE. No, you don't, dear. Miss Baby Love is far
from finished. First, a nice powder base —— (*She lavishly dusts
Dolly's face with a powder puff.*)

RITZ. See, Miss Dolly, it's like this. . . . I have a little proposition to make you.

DOLLY. I don't believe, sir . . . that I care to hear it.

RITZ. (*Laughs, then, producing a very fat envelope from his inside pocket, squats in front of Dolly.*) You don't have to listen
. . . just use your eyes. Fifteen hundred dollars. (*He takes a
thick sheaf of bills out of envelope and begins to count them out
in a little pile on the ground.*)

MISS BABY LOVE. (*Arrested by the sight of money, she eyes
Ritz with a greedy shrewdness.*) Tell me, dearie . . . haven't we
met before?

RITZ. (*Glancing at her while continuing to count his money.*)
Can't remember the pleasure. (*Offering his hand.*) Dr. Morris
Ritz, chemical engineer. (*She extends her hand. He kisses it.*)

MISS BABY LOVE. (*Pointing to herself.*) Miss Baby Love Dallas,
beautician. (*Shapes her lips in a kiss to him, then moves around
to his* R.) All the same, I never forget a face—especially if it's my
type.

RITZ. All right, Miss Dolly, there it is. (*Pointing to money he
has counted out.*) And mind you, this is merely a down payment.
There's a firm in Chicago willing to pay a very substantial amount
for your dropsy recipe.

DOLLY. (*Looking at money.*) I have nothing to sell.

RITZ. (*Looks at her suspiciously, then looks at Miss Baby Love,
he stands up, carefully protecting his money by putting his foot
over it, then, in an idealistic manner as he starts this speech, Miss
Baby Love goes to her case and paws around in it, looking for a
magazine.*) What about the human race? Your dropsy cure, why,

it may be the very stuff to remedy this old planet's ills. Have you the right to keep that from your fellow human beings?

CATHERINE. Anybody wants our dropsy . . . all they got to do is send us a dollar's worth of money order.

DOLLY. Did . . . did my sister send you on this errand?

RITZ. That good lady. I'm afraid our set-up has been liquidated. I'm all for you . . . giving her the air. Why share our profits with her? (*During last speech Miss Baby Love, having found her magazine, hurries over to stage* R., *so that she may not be noticed by the others as she hurries through pages looking for something. On words "giving her the air," she steps forward triumphantly brandishing magazine.*)

MISS BABY LOVE. That's who you are. . . . I told you I had a keen memory. So I'm remembering the latest issue of True Life Detective. . . . (*She taps magazine.*) It contains a very interesting picture and information about a reward. (*With a wink.*) Get me, dearie?

RITZ. (*Bending, he scoops up money and stuffs it in his pocket, then, and with his nervous-tick laugh.*) Some little joker. A girl like you ought not to be on the loose; what you need is a chaperone. (*He comes toward her menacingly but she circles him and runs in the direction of the others. Offstage* R., *above the other voices, we hear two people calling, they are the Barber and the Baker's Wife.*)

BARBER. Yoo-hoo . . . yoo-hoo. Miss Dolly . . . where are you?

BAKER'S WIFE. Miss Dolly. . . . Hello-o! Hello! (*They enter from* R. *through the grass.*)

BARBER. (*Stopping dead at the sight of Ritz, pointing.*) There he is . . . the crook: don't let him get away . . . (*Ritz stampedes directly toward Barber and Baker's Wife, who cower before him. Having stopped them, he exits* R., *running through the grass. Barber, shouting after him.*) Stop, thief! Stop!

MISS BABY LOVE. (*As soon as Ritz is distracted by Barber, Miss Baby Love goes to her case, locks it, leaving magazine on mound. As Ritz exits, she picks up her case, calls after him and follows him off.*) Wait for me, dearie. I'll give you a lift in my automobile

CATHERINE. (*Who has picked up the magazine left by Miss Baby Love, now moves to Barber and Baker's Wife, showing them reward notice.*) He's wanted in six states. There was a thousand-dollar reward for him. We done lost it.

BARBER. More than that, I'm afraid.

DOLLY. What do you mean, Mr. La Grand?

BAKER'S WIFE. (*Going to Dolly, gently.*) Miss Dolly, he stole Verena's money.

BARBER. All of it.

DOLLY. (*Stricken, and as she stiffly sits down on mound.*) Oh. (*Catherine picks up quilt she has slept on, starts up the tree.*)

BAKER'S WIFE. (*Reprovingly.*) Not all of it, Amos.

BARBER. Why quibble, my dear? At any rate all her cash: five thousand eight hundred dollars . . . so I'm told. (*Judge's voice again sounds through the woods in a yodel.*) *What* on earth is that?

CATHERINE. Judge Charlie Cool . . . that's our signal. (*She gives Judge his answering holler, then climbs up into tree-house.*)

BARBER. Just like the jungle . . . isn't it thrilling? (*Then to Dolly, as though there has been no interruption, and with a relish for his tale.*) There you are, my dear . . . that's what happens when you leave money lying around. And of all people, Verena Talbo. Here we thought she trotted to the bank with every dime came her way. But no. Kept it all in her office-safe . . . didn't trust a bank. And so this morning there it was . . . the door of her safe swung *wide* open. Well, sir, when she saw that she trotted right over to the Lola Hotel, only to discover that her esteemed colleague had checked out. . . . I should say. When they brought her to from her *first* faint, she fainted all over again. Five thousand eight . . .

DOLLY. (*Rising and whirling on Barber, her voice pained, emotional.*) Don't. Don't enjoy misery. Theft. Deceit. I can hear it in your voice . . . that wretched pleasure. (*She hesitates, it is almost a stutter, then:*) Perhaps Verena did not trust the bank. But . . . I don't know why . . . she trusted Dr. Ritz. That is what she is suffering . . . the loss of trust. (*Sitting on mound.*) Once, years ago, my sister loved someone; she doesn't know I know it, but I do. It was Laura Murphy . . . maybe you remember her, she worked a while in the post office. It was a great blow when Laura met that whiskey salesman, married him. I couldn't criticize her. . . . It was only fitting if she loved the man. Still, those are the two people I feel Verena has trusted . . . Laura and . . . and

54

Dr. Ritz. And both of them . . . well, it would take the heart out of anyone.

BAKER'S WIFE. Never mind Amos, Miss Dolly: he chatters on . . . but he is your friend, we did come as your friends. (*Moving to L. of Dolly, sits.*) And I want to say: come home, Miss Dolly. (*Earnestly, matter-of-factly, and looking directly at Dolly, who is also looking at her.*) It sets such a poor example for the town, two sisters quarreling, one of them leaving home in a public manner. Leading citizens have to behave themselves, otherwise the entire place falls to pieces.

BARBER. You should see . . . crowds like Saturday night. And the Reverend's wife stopping everybody on the street to tell how she's sworn out her warrant for your arrest because Catherine bit her.

CATHERINE. Bit that old buzzard! I'd be brushing my teeth till doomsday.

BARBER. Oh dear . . . and I'd so hoped it was true. I do relish a little excitement . . . though it does make my throat quite dry. I wonder, do you have a drink of water? (*He goes to base of tree and extends his hand, while watching and listening to the others. Catherine, in full view of the audience, but in such a manner that Barber does not see her, begins to fill an empty jellyjar with water from goldfish bowl.*)

BAKER'S WIFE. (*To Dolly, diffidently.*) And is that your . . . your tree-house, Miss Dolly?

DOLLY. (*So concentrated she has not heard this question, then, to Baker's Wife.*) But is she really sick . . . my sister? I've never known her to be.

CATHERINE. Never a day. (*Handing down jellyjar of water to Barber.*) Here y'are, Amos.

BARBER. (*Taking jar from Catherine and taking a long drink.*) Only *where* did it come from? It tastes so sort of . . . fishy.

CATHERINE. That's just some of Buster's water. (*Nonchalantly wiggling her finger in goldfish bowl as Barber watches her.*) Getting mighty shallow in there . . . huh, Buster?

BARBER. (*Puts down glass, and with a stabbing look at Catherine.*) Thank you.

DOLLY. (*To Baker's Wife, with intense concern.*) But is it so what Amos said . . . about my sister fainting?

BARBER. (*Moving down to Dolly.*) Verena's not the one to come

55

down with anything an aspirin couldn't fix. I remember when she wanted to re-arrange the cemetery, kick everybody out of their graves and put up some kind of fancy mausoleum to house herself and all you Talbos. Poor old Mrs. Twotoes said to me: Amos, don't you think Verena Talbo is the most *morbid* person in town, contemplating such a big tomb for herself? And I said, No . . . the only thing morbid was that she was willing to spend the money when not for an instant did she believe she was ever going to die.

BAKER'S WIFE. I don't know as I think that story is in good taste, Amos. (*Rising.*) Before you talk yourself into a grave, kindly lead me back to town. . . . (*On words "back to town" Collin, Maude and Judge enter together from the rear* L. *They are laughing, as though at some story the Judge has been telling them.*)

JUDGE. (*As they enter, and with a cheerful flourish.*) No elopement, no elopement. You can rest your soul, Catherine. They just were wading in the river. . . .

CATHERINE. Wading? How? (*She snorts.*) Buck-naked?

DOLLY. (*To Catherine.*) Hush now. Now hush. That's not a bit pleasant.

MAUDE. (*Shyly.*) It's God's own truth, Miss Dolly. We were only wading. (*Then gazing around at group.*) I want to ask a favor of you-all . . . please don't say to anyone about my being here: you know how my daddy is. . . . (*She looks with especial significance at Barber.*)

BARBER. (*With a hand to his chest.*) Why roll your eyes at me? Mercy knows, I'm no gossip.

COLLIN. Aw, tell her old man. Let him lump it. When I join the navy, Maude can be one of my dependents.

CATHERINE. (*Drily.*) Well, Dollyheart . . . looks like we're gonna be living on less and less. (*Judge goes to fireplace.*)

DOLLY. (*To Maude.*) Don't fret, child. You go along to town with Amos and Mrs. County. (*Maude nods, helped by Collin, she gathers and straps her schoolbooks. Barber moves toward the grass, they are followed by Dolly and Baker's Wife. Catherine remains in tree-house.*)

BAKER'S WIFE. (*To Dolly, as they walk toward the grass* R.) I won't have an easy breath till I know you're safe and home. (*She stops, faces Dolly, then, quietly, warmly, others stop to listen.*) We can't live in trees . . . maybe some of us would like to, but none of us can. (*With tender intensity.*) Be forgiven. Forgive.

56

(*She kisses Dolly on the cheek.*) Good-bye, dear. (*Joined by Collin and Maude, Barber and Baker's Wife exit* R. *through the grass. Dolly waves.*)

CATHERINE. (*Calling.*) Collin . . . where you think you headed?

COLLIN. (*As he exits.*) I'm going to walk them far as the road.

CATHERINE. See you get back here without no more wadin'. (*There is a diminishing of light—as though clouds were passing overhead. Particularly there is a sense of shadowiness in the tree where Catherine sits now with an invisible quietness.*)

JUDGE. (*Looking up at sky.*) Clouding over. . . . I doubt it will rain, though. (*Lifting his foot, wiggling his ankle.*) Rain-clouds start a hurting in my ankle.

DOLLY. (*Her back to Judge.*) He stole my sister's money.

JUDGE. (*After a puzzled moment.*) Amos did?

DOLLY. Her friend from Chicago. The Doctor. (*Judge emits a low, impressed whistle, and moves toward her. Dolly looks at him, then.*) Should I go home? . . . Mrs. County thinks so . (*Then facing audience.*) Be forgiven. Forgive. Except . . . forgiving . . . that for me has always meant giving way . . . losing myself until I don't know I can do what you said we must.

JUDGE. (*Coming toward her.*) What we must . . . ?

DOLLY. Find out who we truly are. That is what you said. More than likely . . . I would discover that I am no one.

JUDGE. You are very much someone.

DOLLY. (*Smiling sadly.*) A spirit? Well, I think spirits are silly things, ghostly things. (*With a radiant widening of her voice.*) I want to shed . . . like the leaves that fall and show the eternal shape and person of the tree. I want to be seen as this person . . . for Verena to see this woman that I am: and if she can forgive her, and be forgiven by her, then that is true and right. . . .

JUDGE. (*Stepping a little to Dolly and gazing at her as though she were new to him.*) Miss Dolly, would you marry me?

DOLLY. (*With lowered head.*) I told you last night . . . I have not earned the privilege of giving answers.

JUDGE. Last night?

DOLLY. (*Blushing.*) Oh . . . then that isn't what you meant?

JUDGE. I didn't know last night that you were anyone who could be married. I kissed you . . . (*He gently puts his finger on her forehead, marking place where he has kissed her.*) but we did not

57

touch. Because last night I had not seen . . . this woman. (*She lifts her head. They are posed, steadily regarding one another. At this moment Collin and Maude, Barber and Baker's Wife have reappeared in the grass* R. *with a silent rush, a sudden starkness.*)

BARBER. (*Anxiously.*) May I speak to you a moment, Judge? (*They meet for a whispered conference under the tree—which Catherine, leaning over the edge of the tree-house, attempts to overhear.*)

DOLLY. (*Tensely.*) Mrs. County . . . why have you all come back?

BAKER'S WIFE. (*Approaching her, followed by Maude and Collin.*) Get your things, Miss Dolly: you must leave at once . . . down to the river and out through the back woods . . .

COLLIN. We're pretty well surrounded . . . they've made a kind of horseshoe . . . with men on either side of the grass . . . and up on the road, when we got there we saw Big Eddie Stover and the Sheriff . . .

MAUDE. They've got guns, Miss Dolly . . .

COLLIN. We had to come back here keeping down low in the grass. There's a full half-circle of them out there . . . waiting.

DOLLY. (*She turns, walks thoughtfully toward moss-mound, then.*) Waiting for what?

COLLIN. (*As he comes toward her.*) For nightfall, I figure. Or maybe more fellows. (*A brief silence. They all join grouping around Dolly, at mound* L. *Catherine is still in tree-house.*)

JUDGE. (*Quietly.*) Well . . . you know the situation, Miss Dolly. We can pull out or . . .

DOLLY. (*Looking away from everyone.*) To stay . . . the right to stay. (*She sits on mound.*) It is mine, as much as my medicine, as much as the tree: I cannot let them take it. (*Pause, then.*) But please, the rest of you . . . it isn't your responsibility.

BAKER'S WIFE. It is that, Miss Dolly. A thing like this, we've all got to see it through. (*As if asking for agreement.*) Amos? (*Amos nods.*) Maude? (*Maude looks for a moment desperate, and then, biting her underlip, nods.*)

JUDGE. (*In a businesslike, even military, manner as he moves* R.) Now listen to me. I've got a rifle . . . but you'd better, everybody, get a load of rocks . . . all you can carry . . . and sticks. We've got to be able to defend ourselves.

DOLLY. (*As others scurry about obeying Judge's commands,
rising.*) Not rocks. Rocks can hurt people. We mustn't do that.
CATHERINE. What about eggs? Nothing like a good cozy egg.
I got way over a dozen here.
JUDGE. All right then . . . haul yourselves into the tree . . .
scatter out on the branches. . . . (*Chattering as they climb,
everyone goes to find his tree-roost.*)
BARBER. I'm *deathly* afraid of height.
BAKER'S WIFE. (*Who is behind Barber.*) Keep on going, Amos.
I'll catch you if you fall.
BARBER. One thing I've tried all my life not to be is a *roughneck.*
(*Judge, on guard, moves to* L., *watching.*)
CATHERINE. (*Like a hawker, and as she dispenses eggs.*) Get
your ammunition here. Eggs. Fresh eggs. Get 'em while they last.
. . . (*She begins happily to partly hum, partly sing.*) Sister Mary
wore, Sister Mary wore three links of chain, ev'ry link was Jesus'
name, I ain't gonna grieve, gonna grieve my Lord, ain't gonna
grieve, gonna grieve, my Lord, ain't gonna grieve, gonna grieve
my Lord, my Lord no more. (*Maude and Collin shinny out on
tree and settle on a far right branch. Dolly, Catherine and Baker's
Wife are in tree-house itself. Barber straddles a branch above tree-
house. Judge remains on the ground, pacing.*)
DOLLY. (*To Catherine.*) Sing right out. Let them hear us. (*Then
suddenly singing herself.*)
>On the tallest tree in Paradise,
>(*Dolly noticing that Judge has turned to listen to her, shyly
>lowers her head and her voice as she continues.*)
>Christians call it the tree of life . . .
>(*Catherine embraces her and joins her, full-voice.*)
>I ain't gonna grieve, gonna grieve my Lord,
>Ain't gonna grieve, gonna grieve my Lord,
>Ain't gonna grieve, gonna grieve my Lord,
>My Lord no more.

EVERYONE. (*The next stanza is sung all together, and the lighting, as they sing, dwindles like a slowly deflating balloon.*)
>Sister Mary wore, Sister Mary wore three links of chain,
>Ev'ry link was Jesus' name—
>I ain't gonna grieve, gonna grieve my Lord,
>Ain't gonna grieve, gonna grieve my Lord,
>Ain't gonna grieve, gonna grieve my Lord,

My Lord no more.

(*Now the scene is in complete darkness. Voices come up stronger.*)

Oh, the tallest tree in Paradise,

Christians call it the tree of life . . .

(*Here the singing abruptly stops—for a flashlight has sparkled in the dark. Then other flashlights, spaced at differing angles, pop their light and focus it on tree. There is a total of fifteen people on stage: Judge and those in the tree account for six of them. The other nine are: Sheriff, the three men known as Big Eddie Stover, Brophy and Sam, and two other men [these can be played in disguise by the actors who appeared previously by Ritz and Post-master], Reverend and Reverend's Wife—all of these, except the ninth person, who is Verena, manipulate flashlights. The lights, then, are all centered on tree—Dolly and her friends blink in the glare, they cannot see who is below them, nor can the audience.*)

VERENA. (*From darkness below fireplace R.*) You fools. (*The flashlights swerve their beams away from tree and directly at Verena. She is therefore the only person on stage whom we see. Her back is to audience, she is dressed in black, is wearing the black hat with the gray dove, and she is leaning on an umbrella cane.*)

COLLIN, MAUDE, BARBER, BAKER'S WIFE. (*Together, and with an intake of breath.*) Verena . . .

VERENA. You, Dolly . . . conniving with these swine to make a mockery of our name.

DOLLY. (*From the darkness.*) Because there are people willing to help each other . . . you call them swine? If that is what you believe, then our name, your name, deserves to be a mockery.

VERENA. (*Precisely, as though it were a clinical opinion.*) You are not yourself.

DOLLY. (*From the darkness.*) But I am. I've taken your advice: stopped hanging my head, I mean. You said it made you dizzy. And not so very long ago . . . you told me you were ashamed of me. Of Catherine. So much of our lives had been lived for you . . . it was painful to realize the waste that had been. Can you know what it is . . . such a feeling of waste?

VERENA. (*Turns and faces the audience, as though she cannot endure the question Dolly has asked: she seems with the lights at her back outlining her, an isolated, desolate figure. Then, in a*) *breaking voice.*) I'm not a well woman. I'm sick . . . I am, Dolly. (*We hear a rustling sound: it is Dolly descending from tree. She is followed by Collin. Several of the flashlights turn on her and follow her progress—the others stay fixed on Verena, toward whom Dolly goes as though she intended to comfort her. Just as Dolly is within a yard of Verena, two men reach out and seize her. There is, from those in the tree, a shocked gasp, an outcry. Verena, coming suddenly to Dolly's defense.*) Stop it . . . don't touch my sister . . . take your hands off her. . . . (*She lifts her umbrella like a weapon.*)

SHERIFF. (*From the darkness, and in a voice like a long echo.*) It's for the law now, Miss Verena. This is for the law to handle. (*Another outcry—then, as the two men try to hold onto Dolly, tumult: the flashlight beams career and tangle in the dark. The climax of this tumult is reached in the sound of a gunshot. The gunshot, a hush, at last a young girl's screams. The flashlights sweep the tree and single out, with a frozen steadiness, Collin, who is standing stage C., facing Sheriff. There is a trance-like stillness about the scene—Collin, with his hands clenched and his head strangely cocked to one side.*)

COLLIN. Don't—don't hurt my Dolly. (*He sways, begins to fall —then, spotted by flashlights, crashes to the ground. Those on the ground converge around him in a circle, with Dolly and the Judge inside it.*)

MAN'S VOICE. (*From inside circle around Collin.*) Is he dead?

DOLLY. (*From inside circle.*) It's Dolly, Collin. Open your eyes, darling. For me . . .

CATHERINE. (*From the tree.*) I never meant a mean word, baby child. I cut out my tongue.

JUDGE. (*From inside circle.*) Stand back. Everybody . . . get back. (*The crowd parts: we see Judge and Dolly hovering over Collin. All flashlights are on them.*)

VERENA. Who fired that shot? Which of you idiots? (*A low murmur among the men—Verena snatches the nearest flashlight and casts its beam over the men's downcast faces. She stops on Big Eddie Stover, whose plump face sags with fear.*)

BIG EDDIE. Well, I never meant to shoot nobody. Was doing my duty, is all.

VERENA. Not all. I hold you responsible, Mr. Stover.

DOLLY. No one is that. No one can be held responsible . . . except ourselves. (*By now everyone has come down from tree.*)
JUDGE. (*As he lifts Collin in his arms.*) We'd better get him to town fast as we can. (*A procession, in which Collin is the center figure, files past Dolly. The flashlights, focused on the ground, swing like lanterns, and music, a memory of the wind in the grass, accompanies their long exit into the* R. *wings. Verena does not quite leave the stage: she waits at the edge of the grass for Dolly. Dolly looks at the tree, bows her head—as curtain falls. She brings her hands together in an attitude of prayer.*)

CURTAIN

ACT II

SCENE 2

Later the same evening. The set is the same as in the first scene of Act I: the exterior of the Talbo house and its dining room. The room is lit by two candles on the dining table and two candles on mantel, the draperies at the windows are drawn, the kitchen door is closed. The door to hallway at U. R. *is open.*
Verena is standing at the windows, her back to audience: She is slightly holding back the draperies and peering out. Judge is seated above the table—Dolly is standing at L. *of it, her back to audience and her hand listlessly endlessly polishing the frame of a chair. Maude is seated in a chair against the wall at far* L. *of stage, below mantel. Presently there is a sound as if coming from upstairs: Dolly looks up at ceiling, as if trying to see into room where Collin lies. Then she looks at cuckoo clock.*

DOLLY. (*Referring to clock.*) It's stopped again. (*To Judge.*) What time is it?
JUDGE. (*Consulting his pocket-watch.*) Twelve . . . a little after. You ought to be home, Maude. You ought to be asleep.
MAUDE. I couldn't anyway. Not without knowing.
DOLLY. Go, Maude; it's better that you do. I will send word.
MAUDE. (*Rising, she walks reluctantly across stage towards* U. R.

62

door, then, turning.) Do you think . . . would Doctor Carter let me see Collin . . . for only a moment? I want to tell him something. (*She is looking at Dolly, and accepts Dolly's silence as answer.*) Then will you tell him for me . . . that it's true what I said about thinking of little things; because all I can think is . . . he must come to my Hallowe'en party. He . . . must. (*She exits u. R. The front door D. R. opens, we see Maude come out carrying her schoolbooks, she gazes for an instant at upper windows of the house, then exits into R. wings. Simultaneous with the moment Maude stands staring at upper windows, Catherine enters the dining-room from u. R. door. She is carrying a tin washbasin, and her sleeves are rolled up. Judge quickly rises at her entrance. Verena, for the first time, looks away from windows and, like Dolly, regards Catherine with an anxious expression.*)

JUDGE. What does Carter say?

CATHERINE. (*Rather gruffly, and as she sails across the room toward kitchen door.*) He says for me to fetch him some more hot water. (*Stops in front of kitchen door, turns back, holds out her hand with palm open.*) There it is. The bullet. (*She walks back to table, as she puts bullet down.*) Old Collin was real brave . . . not one whisper . . . just let Doc Carter dig it out of him; was here in the shoulder. (*Judge reaches for bullet, as if he wanted to examine it, Catherine snatches it up.*) No you don't . . . (*As she exits through kitchen door.*) I'm saving it for that boy to show his children! (*Dolly moves toward Judge—still-faced at first, then with a quiet tearful-laughing relief: there is nothing hysterical about this—rather, it is as though she were immensely exhilarated, Judge smiles at her, holds her. Verena, observing them woodenly, moves round table, puts her hand on back of a chair.*)

VERENA. (*To Judge, with an effort as she moves to mantel L.*) I have something to say to my sister. I could say it more easily if we were alone.

JUDGE. (*Removing his hands from Dolly, and placing them in his pockets, then for a moment pondering Verena as though he were trying to read her mind; at last, as if he'd come to a sudden decision.*) I'm afraid you'll have to put up with me, Miss Verena. I have an interest in the outcome of what you might have to say.

VERENA. (*Coldly.*) I doubt that. How so? (*She waits for his reply. Catherine enters from kitchen and, carrying the washbasin filled with steaming water, hurriedly crosses room and exits out*

u. r. *dining-room door.*) How so, Charlie Cool? (*Then, when there is still no reply forthcoming.*) As a man with a legal background, I'm certain you will appreciate my coming to the point. Frankly . . . you're not a welcome sight to me. My sister could not have gone through with such tommyrot if you had not been . . . if some stronger wilful spiteful person . . . had not been goading her on. So I'll thank you to leave us: it can be no further affair of yours.

DOLLY. But it is. (*As she sits in a chair at* R. *of table.*) Because Judge Cool . . .

JUDGE. (*Leaning his hands on table, looking at Dolly.*) Dolly means that I have asked her to marry me.

VERENA. (*A brief, disbelieving laugh, then.*) That . . . is remarkable. Very. I wouldn't have credited either of you with so much imagination. Or is it that *I* am imagining? Quite likely I am dreaming . . . except that I never have dreams. Or could it be that I only forget them? I suggest this one we all forget.

JUDGE. I'll own up, Verena. I think it is a dream. But a man who doesn't dream is like a man who doesn't sweat: he stores up a lot of poison.

VERENA. (*Has not listened to him, her attention is fixed on Dolly. Then, in a tone of finality.*) I see. You've accepted him.

DOLLY. (*Quietly.*) I thought I would know what was right. But it hasn't happened. Rather, what has happened is . . . I can see now that in a vain self-pitying corner of myself I've always felt that *I alone* knew what was right. Just as you did, Verena. And people who believe they alone are right can do nothing but deliver ultimatums. You made an ultimatum . . . it meant we had to leave this house; and in leaving . . . that was mine to you. And together we made an ultimatum to God; and He answered us . . . He chose Collin. . . . I don't know why, because that bullet was meant for me. I thought . . . to have a life made of my own decisions . . . is that not what we're meant to do?

VERENA. But we have had our lives. Yours has been nothing to despise: you've never been deeply alone, you've never been deeply betrayed. (*Pause.*) I've envied you always.

DOLLY. Is it true, Judge? Have we had our lives?

JUDGE. Not you. Not me.

VERENA. (*She has not taken her eyes off Dolly, has seemed hypnotized by her. She comes toward Dolly, as she touches back of*

64

her chair.) Envied you. I walk through the house . . . nothing is mine. Your rooms, your kitchen, the house is yours . . . I can only knock at the door . . . as I've knocked at the doors of other houses; not often . . . enough to know that now there is no one but you to let me in. Because Dr. Ritz, Morris . . . help me, I loved him, I did. It was—oh, I admit it, that we were kindred spirits. We looked at each other, we saw the same devil: it was . . . merry. But he outsmarted me; I'd known he could, and hoped he wouldn't, and he did, and now . . . (*She begins to slide downward, holding chair with one hand and with other fiercely gripping Dolly's wrist.*) it's too long to be alone, a lifetime. Dolly, Dolly . . . let me live with you, I'm feeling old, I want my sister. (*She is crying, she presses her face against Dolly, who passes a soothing hand over her hair.*) You won't leave me?

DOLLY. I won't leave you. (*She looks at Judge, who has turned his back on them as though he had no right to be there, as though he wished to make himself invisible. Rising, she starts toward him, stops; then.*) Forgive me . . . I want my sister, too. (*Judge, his back still turned, it is as if he does not trust himself to speak. He begins slowly to move toward door of dining room u. r. as Dolly takes a step after him.*) Sometimes . . . you will come to see me? (*Judge does not look at her—it is as though he could not bear it if he did; then, with an agonizing nod, and never once glancing back, he exits u. r.—immediately appearing again at the front door d. r. He walks across sidewalk r. to l. and exits d. l. into wings. Dolly has in a sense followed his exit—she has watched him go out dining-room door; then, as he crosses stage and out l., her whole body gradually turns in direction of his departure and together they move across stage. However Dolly stops as she nears mantel at l. Until he has left the stage there is silence in dining-room. Verena has pulled herself up, is sitting in the chair at r. of table.*)

VERENA. (*As though thinking aloud.*) You've never seen the ocean, have you? (*She waits; Dolly looks at her.*) It is a comforting sight—a wave leaving a shell, a wave taking it back. We could go on a trip—the two of us . . . or Catherine may come if you like. I've considered selling a few . . . a few properties. It could be a long trip. We might take a boat. I could show you the ocean.

DOLLY. The ocean?—that would only be another tree-house, Verena, something we should not allow ourselves. There is so much to be lived—and my life is here. You were wrong—we've not had our lives.

CATHERINE. (*Appears in dining-room door* U. R., *rolling down her sleeves and with the look of having finished a job, as she enters.*) Doc Carter's leaving now. . . . Collin's asleep.

VERENA. (*Softly.*) Please, then, Catherine, turn down the lights.

CATHERINE. (*As she crosses room to mantel. When there, she snuffs downstage candle.*) I left Buster, Dollyheart . . . left him there in the tree. I best go get him 'fore he catches his death.

DOLLY. It's not such a cold night. We'll go tomorrow. We must take our spades . . . I want to get enough dropsy herbs to see us through the winter.

CATHERINE. Who's gonna carry all that? You know the worries I have with my back . . . and Collin, that boy's not gonna be in any condition awhile yet. . . . (*Moves to candle upstage on mantel and snuffs it.*)

DOLLY. We could hire somebody. Or take in a new partner. If he would accept . . . I think we should make the Judge a partner.

VERENA. (*To Dolly—they are several feet apart, at opposite ends of table.*) May I . . . may I come with you, too? I would like to help . . . if you will let me. (*Dolly looks at Verena—starts to go toward her, pauses, holds out her hand, it is a gesture of welcome and, as she lifts her hand, as Verena advances to accept it, music begins. Together, Dolly and Verena move toward dining-room door* U. R. *Catherine, watching them, moves to above table. As the sisters start out she snuffs candle* L. *on table. The scrim falls and for a moment we see Catherine sitting in chair at table. She then snuffs candle* R. *on table. As the music rises, we see the outside of the house glow, then darken.*)

CURTAIN

66

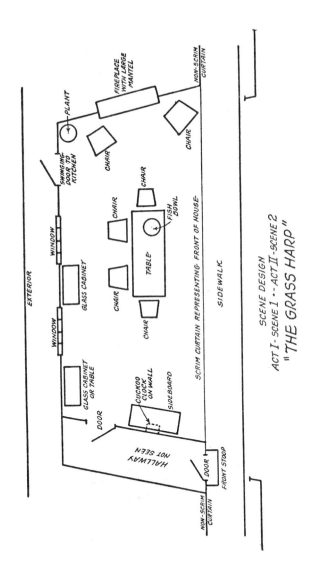

SCENE DESIGN
ACT I - SCENE 1 - ACT II - SCENE 2
"THE GRASS HARP"

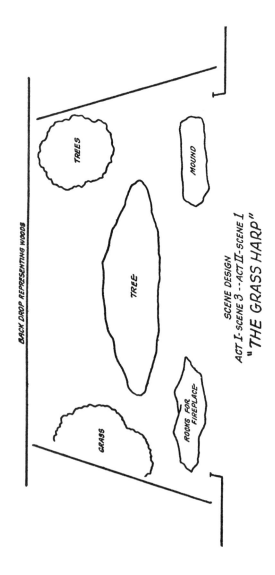

BACK DROP REPRESENTING WOODS

TREES

MOUND

TREE

GRASS

ROCKS FOR FIREPLACE

SCENE DESIGN
ACT I- SCENE 3 -- ACT II-SCENE I
"THE GRASS HARP"

PROPERTY PLOT

ACT I—SCENE 1—INTERIOR

Furniture:

1 oval dining table
6 chairs (4 at table, 2 on either side of mantel)
1 sideboard
1 mantelpiece with fireplace in L. flat
1 small cabinet U. R. corner
1 wrought iron shelf piece—between windows

Hangings:

Drapes on windows to draw closed
2 gilt moulded valances

Dressing:

Cuckoo clock on R. flat above sideboard
Green velour mantelshelf cover—gold tasseled
Mirror above mantelpiece
Red velour table cover—on table
1 picture, 2 paintings
2 double wrought iron plant holders
Wood basket with logs—above mantel on floor
4 pots, pans on kitchen backing
2 candlesticks with candles and shades on mantelshelf
2 candlesticks with candles and shades on sideboard R.
Bric-a-brac to dress sideboard, small table shelf piece, mantel, and
  shelves above doors

Props:

Goldfish bowl with large fish on dining table
Jigsaw puzzle, partially complete picture fixed on board, loose pieces
  on board, 8 loose pieces on D. S. end table
Small mirror on table
Cigarettes and matches—Collin
Elaborate bowl with roses off L.—Dolly
Silver settings for 6—drawer sideboard
Linen tablecloth—lower shelf sideboard
6 linen napkins—lower shelf sideboard

Candy paper bag with jelly beans—lower shelf sideboard
6 dinner plates—lower shelf sideboard
6 water glasses—lower shelf sideboard
6 cups and saucers—lower shelf sideboard
3 letters in envelopes—Dolly off L.
Small paper wrapped parcel—Verena off L.
Small box kitchen matches—sideboard
Small silver dinner bell—sideboard
Platter with 6 pieces fried chicken, chicken livers, and silver tongs—
    off L.—Catherine
1 vegetable dish and serving spoons—off L.—Catherine
Plate with cake and cake knife off L.—Catherine
Fountain pen—Ritz, off L.
Prescription pad—Ritz off L.

Hand Props:

Market bag—Reverend's Wife
Green eye shade, spectacles, sleeve covers, Postmaster
Silver Sheriff's star, cartridge belt and hip holster, warrant, pistol in
holster, Sheriff

ACT I—SCENE 3

Dressing:

6 grass set pieces—stage R.
Log mound—stage L.
Fireplace rock piece—stage R.

Hand Props:

2 shoe boxes—raft
1 sugar sack R. of tree
Wooden box as seat—raft
Small wooden barrel as seat—raft
Wooden box with twigs and wood—above tree R.
Fish bowl and fish (duplicate of 1—1)—Catherine off L.
Man's wallet with $43.55. Bills and coins—Dolly
Cigarettes and matches—Collin
Hunting rifle—Judge, off R.
2 dead squirrels rigged to hang from belt· Judge
Apples, oranges, cupcakes, fried chicken in shoe box—raft
Cigarettes and matches—Judge
2 scrap quilts—raft
Sticks and twigs for fire—above log L.
2 bottles blackberry wine—raft
4 tin cups—raft

Gold nugget pocket size—Judge
2 empty jelly glasses—raft
Pocket knife and wood for whittling—Collin
Rope for knot tying—Collin

Effect:
Off stage pistol shot—stage R.

ACT II—SCENE 1

Props:
3 school books held together by strap—Maude—off R.
Salesman's suitcase painted red with golden stars, with pictures of
Clara Bow, Jean Harlow, "Sweetheart Cosmetics" lettered in silver
both sides—off R.
Rhinestone-studded mirror with handle, large perfume atomizer, large
powder puff, cosmetic jars, boxes, tubes, True Detective magazine—
Miss Baby Love—in suitcase
Large envelope with money (bills)—Ritz off R.
24 prop. eggs in box—raft
Revolver and blanks—practical—sure fire—Brophy
Holster and belt for above—Brophy

ACT II—SCENE 2

Furniture:
Same as 1—1

Drapes:
Closed

Dressing:
Same
4 candles lighted
Clear all dishes and linen from 1—1

Props:
Pocket watch and chain—Judge
Tin washbasin—Catherine off R.
Bullet head—Catherine—off R.
Candle snuffer on mantel

NEW PLAYS

★ **BENGAL TIGER AT THE BAGHDAD ZOO by Rajiv Joseph.** The lives of two American Marines and an Iraqi translator are forever changed by an encounter with a quick-witted tiger who haunts the streets of war-torn Baghdad. "[A] boldly imagined, harrowing and surprisingly funny drama." *–NY Times.* "Tragic yet darkly comic and highly imaginative." *–CurtainUp.* [5M, 2W] ISBN: 978-0-8222-2565-2

★ **THE PITMEN PAINTERS by Lee Hall, inspired by a book by William Feaver.** Based on the triumphant true story, a group of British miners discover a new way to express themselves and unexpectedly become art-world sensations. "Excitingly ambiguous, in-the-moment theater." *–NY Times.* "Heartfelt, moving and deeply politicized." *–Chicago Tribune.* [5M, 2W] ISBN: 978-0-8222-2507-2

★ **RELATIVELY SPEAKING by Ethan Coen, Elaine May and Woody Allen.** In TALKING CURE, Ethan Coen uncovers the sort of insanity that can only come from family. Elaine May explores the hilarity of passing in GEORGE IS DEAD. In HONEYMOON MOTEL, Woody Allen invites you to the sort of wedding day you won't forget. "Firecracker funny." *–NY Times.* "A rollicking good time." *–New Yorker.* [8M, 7W] ISBN: 978-0-8222-2394-8

★ **SONS OF THE PROPHET by Stephen Karam.** If to live is to suffer, then Joseph Douaihy is more alive than most. With unexplained chronic pain and the fate of his reeling family on his shoulders, Joseph's health, sanity, and insurance premium are on the line. "Explosively funny." *–NY Times.* "At once deep, deft and beautifully made." *–New Yorker.* [5M, 3W] ISBN: 978-0-8222-2597-3

★ **THE MOUNTAINTOP by Katori Hall.** A gripping reimagination of events the night before the assassination of the civil rights leader Dr. Martin Luther King, Jr. "An ominous electricity crackles through the opening moments." *–NY Times.* "[A] thrilling, wild, provocative flight of magical realism." *–Associated Press.* "Crackles with theatricality and a humanity more moving than sainthood." *–NY Newsday.* [1M, 1W] ISBN: 978-0-8222-2603-1

★ **ALL NEW PEOPLE by Zach Braff.** Charlie is 35, heartbroken, and just wants some time away from the rest of the world. Long Beach Island seems to be the perfect escape until his solitude is interrupted by a motley parade of misfits who show up and change his plans. "Consistently and sometimes sensationally funny." *–NY Times.* "A morbidly funny play about the trendy new existential condition of being young, adorable, and miserable." *–Variety.* [2M, 2W] ISBN: 978-0-8222-2562-1

DRAMATISTS PLAY SERVICE, INC.
440 Park Avenue South, New York, NY 10016 212-683-8960 Fax 212-213-1539
postmaster@dramatists.com www.dramatists.com